Dubai

WHAT'S NEW | WHAT'S ON | WHAT'S BEST

www.timeout.com/dubai

Contents

Published by Time Out Guides Ltd
Universal House
251 Tottenham Court Road
London W1T 7AB
Tel: + 44 (0)20 7813 3000
Fax: + 44 (0)20 7813 6001
Email: guides@timeout.com
www.timeout.com

Managing Director Peter Fiennes
Editorial Director Ruth Jarvis
Business Manager Dan Allen
Editorial Manager Holly Pick
Management Accountants Margaret Wright, Clare Turner

Time Out Guides is a wholly owned subsidiary of Time Out Group Ltd.

© Time Out Group Ltd
Chairman & Founder Tony Elliott
Chief Executive Officer David King
Chief Operating Officer Aksel Van der Wal
Group Financial Director Paul Rakkar
Group General Manager/Director Nichola Coulthard
Time Out Communications Ltd MD David Pepper
Time Out International Ltd MD Cathy Runciman
Time Out Magazine Ltd Publisher/Managing Director Mark Elliot
Group Commercial Director Graeme Tottle
Group IT Director Simon Chappell
Group Marketing Director Andrew Booth
Time Out GCC
Publisher Zoë Cooper-Clark
Group Editor Ross Brown

Time Out and the Time Out logo are trademarks of Time Out Group Ltd.

This edition first published in Great Britain in 2011 by Ebury Publishing
A Random House Group Company
Company information can be found on www.randomhouse.co.uk
Random House UK Limited Reg. No. 954009
10 9 8 7 6 5 4 3 2

Distributed in the US by Publishers Group West
Distributed in Canada by Publishers Group Canada

For further distribution details, see www.timeout.com

ISBN: 978-1-84670-253-2

A CIP catalogue record for this book is available from the British Library.

Printed and bound in India by Replika Press Pvt. Ltd.

MIX
Paper from
responsible sources
FSC® C016779

The Random House Group Limited supports The Forest Stewardship Council (FSC®), the leading
international forest certification organisation. Our books carrying the FSC label are printed on FSC® certified
paper. FSC is the only forest certification scheme endorsed by the leading environmental organisations,
including Greenpeace. Our paper procurement policy can be found at www.randomhouse.co.uk/environment

Dubai Shortlist

The **Time Out Dubai Shortlist** is one of a new series of guides that draws on Time Out's background as a magazine publisher to keep you current with everything that's going on in town. As well as Dubai's key sights and the best of its eating, drinking, arts and leisure options, the guide picks out the most exciting venues to have recently opened and gives a full calendar of annual events. It also includes features on the important news, trends and openings, all compiled by locally based editors and writers. Whether you're visiting Dubai for the first time in your life or just for the first time this year, you'll find the *Time Out Dubai Shortlist* contains everything you need to know, in a portable and easy-to-use format.

The guide divides central Dubai into six areas, each containing listings for Sights & Museums, Eating & Drinking, Shopping, Nightlife and Arts & Leisure, and maps pinpointing their locations. At the front of the book are chapters rounding up these scenes city-wide, and giving a shortlist of our overall picks in a variety of categories. We also include itineraries for days out, plus essentials such as transport information and hotels.

Our listings give phone numbers as dialled within the UAE. The international code for Dubai is 00971. To call from outside Dubai follow this with the number given, dropping the initial '0'. Some listed numbers (starting with 050 or 055) are mobiles.

We have noted price categories by using one to four dollar signs ($-$$$$), representing budget, moderate, expensive and luxury. Major credit cards are accepted unless otherwise stated.

All our listings are double-checked, but places do occasionally close or change their hours or prices, so it's a good idea to call a venue before visiting. While every effort has been made to ensure accuracy, the publishers cannot accept responsibility for any errors that this guide may contain.

Venues are marked on the maps using symbols numbered according to their order within the chapter and colour-coded according to the type of venue they represent:

❶ Sights & Museums
❶ Eating & Drinking
❶ Shopping
❶ Nightlife
❶ Arts & Leisure

Map key	
Major sight or landmark	▮
Hospital or college	▮
Railway station	▮
Park	▮
Water	▮
Motorway	▬
Major road	—
Main road tunnel	– –
Airport	✈
Area name	**DEIRA**

Time Out **Dubai** Shortlist

EDITORIAL
Editor Georgina Wilson-Powell
Assistant Editors Vineetha Menon,
Simon Coppock
Proofreaders Jenny Hewett, Drew Jones

DESIGN
Art Director Scott Moore
Art Editor Pinelope Kourmouzoglou
Senior Designer Kel Ishimaru
Designer (Dubai) Lucy McMurray
Group Commercial Designer Jodi Sher

Picture Editor Jael Marschner
Picture Editor (Dubai) Adam Wilson
Picture Desk Assistant/Researcher
Ben Rowe

ADVERTISING
New Business & Commercial Director
Mark Phillips
International Advertising Manager
Kasimir Berger
International Sales Executive
Charlie Sokol

ADVERTISING DUBAI
Group Commercial Director Walid Zok
Advertising Director Gareth Lloyd-Jones
Senior Advertising Manager
MIchael Smith
Advertising Manager Linda Murphy
Advertising Manager Farrah Phillips

MARKETING
Senior Publishing Brand Manager
Luthfa Begum
Guides Marketing Manager
Colette Whitehouse
Group Commercial Art Director
Anthony Huggins

PRODUCTION
Group Production Manager
Brendan McKeown
Production Controller Katie Mulhern
Production Manager (Dubai)
Subramanian A C
Production Co-ordinator (Dubai)
Balasubramanian P

CONTRIBUTORS
This guide was researched and written by Andy Buchan and the writers of *Time Out Dubai*.

PHOTOGRAPHY
All photography ITP.
Cover photography The Burj Khalifa. Credit: Gavin Hellier/Photolibrary.com.

MAPS
Maps by JS Graphics Ltd (john@jsgraphics.co.uk). Maps are based on material supplied by Netmaps.

About Time Out

Founded in 1968, Time Out has expanded from humble London beginnings into the leading resource for those wanting to know what's happening in the world's greatest cities. As well as our influential what's-on weeklies in London, New York and Chicago, we publish more than a dozen other listings magazines in cities as varied as Beijing and Mumbai. The magazines established Time Out's trademark style: sharp writing, informed reviewing and bang up-to-date inside knowledge of every scene.

Time Out made the natural leap into travel guides in the 1980s with the City Guide series, which now extends to over 50 destinations around the world. Written and researched by expert local writers and generously illustrated with original photography, the full-size guides cover a larger area than our Shortlist guides and include many more venue reviews, along with additional background features and a full set of maps.

Throughout this rapid growth, the company has remained proudly independent, still owned by Tony Elliott four decades after he started Time Out London as a single fold-out sheet of A5 paper. This independence extends to the editorial content of all our publications, this Shortlist included. No establishment has been featured because it has advertised, and no payment has influenced any of our reviews. And, for our critics, there's definitely no such thing as a free lunch: all restaurants and bars are visited and reviewed anonymously, and Time Out always picks up the bill.

For more about the company, see www.timeout.com.

Don't Miss

An indulgent new menu
for the sophisticated in taste

cavalli club
RESTAURANT & LOUNGE

Abra station

Sights & Museums

Dubai's cultural cachet has never been particularly strong and over the last few years, it has suffered healthy derision from Westerners who haven't fled the European or American recession to enjoy the tax-free sand, sun and sea lifestyle here. Its history isn't rich with invasions and it hasn't birthed cultural movements in the way that Europe has, but it does have sights (and a couple of museums) to see. Visitors should put any scorn aside and appreciate Dubai as living history. The 'sights' might not appear as valid as something ruined or covered in ivy, but in under 30 years, an entire metropolis has risen from nothing. This city is full of diverse architecture, even more diverse nationalities and is still very

much in the process of being settled. The sights here are full of the living, not the dead, and the city is in a constant state of flux and evolution. A visitor who last arrived five years ago would have trouble, today, navigating some parts of town and wouldn't even have heard of others. Surely that's history in the making.

Old Dubai

Some people might snort at the thought of an 'old' Dubai and yes, compared to most other cities around the world, nothing in Dubai is 'old'. However, compared to the recently constructed Dubai Marina (see p140), life around the Creek hasn't changed much since the first skyscraper went up in 1978. Old

Dubai comprises Deira, Garhoud and Bur Dubai – the Creek is a bustling centre for boat-based trade, with the humble wooden dhows mostly unchanged for decades. Head down to these locales and get lost in a city that feels 'foreign' even to those who have lived in Dubai for years. Home to the first wave of South Asian immigrants, Deira still fields some of the most authentic restaurants – although don't go expecting five-star hospitality. Bur Dubai is also home to the Dubai Museum (see p81), where visitors can learn about the fishing village Dubai used to be.

New and newer

Dubai's progress is clearly marked out as a timeline that runs parallel to Jumeirah Beach (see p114), with its past in Deira and its future up at Dubai Marina (see p140). The main artery of the city, Sheikh Zayed Road, pumps the lifeblood of cars and taxis up and down the 40-kilometre stretch. At one end stands Jumeirah Emirates Towers (see p168), twin skyscrapers which once were the only thing interrupting the desert's horizon. Now, they're a part of the modern, sleek elegance of Dubai International Financial Centre (DIFC). What was once the centre of 'new' Dubai is now only one end of the city, as the centre continues to move further and further south. A few years ago 'Downtown', also known as 'Old Town' (no irony intended) was just a large hole in the ground. Now, it's home to the world's tallest building Burj Khalifa (see p102), tallest fountains and largest mall (see p105). Wide pavements and a smattering of street-side cafés give this area a more Western feel and suggest Dubai is finally making some concessions to a population wishing

S H O R T L I S T

Best for a day trip
- Abu Dhabi (see p156)
- Ice Land, Ras Al Khaimah (see p159)

Best for the desert
- Al Ain (see p157)
- Liwa (see p157)

Best for bling
- Burj al Arab (see p172)
- Jumeirah Emirates Towers (see p168)

Best for Mosque-do sights
- Grand Mosque, Abu Dhabi (see p156)
- Jumeirah Mosque (see p115)

Best animal attraction
- Al Ain Wildlife Park (see p157)

Best waterpark
- Aquaventure, Atlantis Hotel (see p155)
- Wild Wadi, Jumeirah Beach Hotel (see p122)

Best for a sunset view
- Burj Khalifa (see p102)
- Madinat Jumeirah (see p136)
- Marina Walk (see p140)
- Sunset Beach (see p126)

Best for a ringside seat
- Armani Hotel (see p169)
- More, Dubai Mall (see p103)
- Souk al Bahar (see p103)

Best creek experience
- Abra crossing point, Bur Dubai (see p80)
- Bateaux Dubai (see p85)

Best for haggling
- Gold Souk (see p65)
- Karama markets (see p87)
- Spice Souk (see p65)

DON'T MISS

Dubai Marina

DON'T MISS

to use environmentally friendly public transport and their own feet, rather than fast cars.

Further south still (20 minutes away by car) lies what is known locally now as 'new Dubai'. Dubai Marina and the Jumeirah Beach Residence development have transformed the previously desolate coastline into a bustling new hub. Now visitors can enjoy a jaunt down The Walk (see p140), a kilometre-long strip of alfresco restaurants, opposite (but sadly not in sight of) the beach, complete with five-star hotels and award-winning bars. Set back from the beach is the marina (and a mall of course), which harbours multi-million pound yachts and more skyscrapers than you can shake a spirit level at. The best way to see these very new sights and get a feel for the shape of the Palm Jumeirah is at one of the sky-high drinking holes, such as Bar 44 in Grosvenor House (see p141).

Getting around

Since September 2009, Dubai has had an above ground metro system, and in typical fashion, it's the longest automated system in the world. Although it has helped congestion slightly, it's still not as quick or as useful as metros in other cities, mainly due to the lack of pavements and pedestrianised areas once you exit the stations. Most malls are now connected to this system on the Red line, which runs parallel to most of Sheikh Zayed Road, before swinging across over to Deira and the airport. If you want to take in the sights, other than those in designer stores, taxis are still your best bet. Flagging one down is the quickest and easiest way, but both malls and hotels have busy taxi ranks. The latter's staff will generally take care of attracting the attention of a taxi driver while you wait in air-conditioned comfort. Queuing at these ranks used to take hours, but an influx of new drivers (and less people in the city thanks to the global recession) has made this a thing of the past. You can order one (04 208 0808) if you're staying out of town, but the booking system can be somewhat unreliable.

To get a good grasp of Dubai's sprawling metropolis, grab a bus tour. The Big Bus Tour (04 340 7709, www.bigbustours.com/eng/dubai) runs open top (and in the summer, air conditioned) double decker buses and operates a hop on/hop off system of 20 stops around the city. Again, many of these are found at malls, so you can combine cultural sightseeing with exercising the credit card. Tours run every day with live commentaries in English and include entry into the Dubai Museum, Sheikh Saeed Al Maktoum House and a dhow boat cruise.

Out of town

Don't be fooled, the UAE is still mostly desert, not shiny skyscrapers, and if you venture more than a kilometre inland, you'll see how little Dubai has really encroached on the shifting sands. The natural landscape has much to offer visitors, from desert safaris to exploring wadis (dry valleys), rock climbing in Fujairah or camping on sand dunes. Both resorts and tour operators can offer these, check out our Worth The Trip chapter for more information (see p156).

Dubai Museum

Home Furniture | Furnishings | Accessories | Wedding Registry

At.mosphere

Eating & Drinking

Dubai is fast-paced, energetic, ever-changing and above all else, it's a great place to grab a bite to eat. Whether you're in the market for glitzy five-star fare, a hideaway restaurant in the backstreets of Karama, or comfort food courtesy of an oh-so-familiar fast food chain, the city caters for all budgets and tastes.

The range and diversity of Dubai's restaurants owes itself to the fact the city is a melting pot of cultures. This, sadly, is often forgotten by visitors, who tend to limit their movements to the comfort of their hotel. However, if you open your mind, peel yourself off the sun lounger and step outside of the lobby, there are many fantastic meals and experiences all lying just a short cab ride away.

High-end dining

Of course, visitors can be forgiven for being drawn to the myriad of Michelin-star names floating about Dubai. Gordon Ramsay, Pierre Gagnaire, Yannick Alléno – Gary Rhodes, Vineet Bhatia, Giorgio Locatelli, and Richard Sandavol are but a few of the chefs who have opened restaurants here. While these renowned chefs are only able to visit once or twice a year, their principles are upheld by prodigious pupils. These individuals – head chefs, sous chefs and pastry chefs – have all received their training in the West's culinary capitals. Not only have they brought to Dubai fresh and innovative ideas, with an emphasis on sustainable and organic produce, they have added a liberal sprinkle of personality to each of their restaurants, ensuring the associated Michelin-star name does not simply become a celebrity brand extension.

In this respect, Dubai's high-end dining scene has never been in a better state. The number of residents with more money than taste has dwindled since the financial crisis, forcing restaurants to raise their game to compete for shrewder, more discerning clientele. Gone are the days where quality took a backseat to opulence and excess – even At.mosphere (see p103) in the Burj Khalifa, which opened with much pomp and ceremony as the world's highest restaurant, surprised many with its simple menu (not a height-related pun in sight) and its sleek, understated interior. Of course, the gawdy, overpriced restaurants remain – a reminder of the heady excess of yesteryear – but Dubai has begun to take its culinary ambitions seriously, and while it is yet to produce its own Michelin-star chef or home-grown restaurant of world renown, it is continuing to import only the best.

Where your food is from

Importation is the name of the game, as far as food in Dubai is concerned. The UAE's sandscape isn't the most hospitable environment in which to grow crops or rear livestock, so it's no surprise that most of Dubai's restaurants import produce from abroad. Stat fans will be interested to know that the UAE imports more than 80 per cent of its food, and in 2010, the country brought in Dhs25.5 billion worth of food. And how, exactly, does this affect the average restaurant-goer? Well, quite simply, the further food travels, the more expensive it's going to

SHORTLIST

Best atmosphere
- La Petite Maison, DIFC (see p97)
- Okku, The Monarch (see p108)

Best budget
- Betawi Café, Karama (see p90)
- Ravi's, Satwa (see p123)

Best brunch
- Saffron, Atlantis (see p154)
- Traiteur, Park Hyatt (see p69)
- Zuma, DIFC (see p100)

Best service
- Reflets par Pierre Gagnaire, Intercontinental Festival City (see p77)

Best chef
- Scott Price at Gordon Ramsey's Verre (see p69)

Best Middle Eastern food
- Al Nafoorah, Jumeirah Emirates Towers (see p97)
- Khan Murjan, Wafi (see p91)

Best Indian
- Aangan, Dhow Palace (see p85)

Best for romance
- Pai Thai, Madinat Jumeirah (see p137)
- Segreto, Madinat Jumeirah (see p137)

Best to impress
- At.mosphere, Burj Khalifa (see p103)
- Neos, The Address Downtown (see p103)

Best backdrop
- Rivington Grill, Souk Al Bahar (see p104)

be once it comes out of the kitchen – something worth noting before converting the cost of the bill back into your home currency.

Budget eating

Of course, you don't always have to empty your wallet in order to fill your stomach. While Dubai has more than its fair share of millionaires, the majority of its population consists of very normal people who can't (and won't) spend a king's ransom on dining out. Dubai is rich with quality budget eateries, most of which can be found in the older ('old' by Dubai standards, that is) parts of the city such as Satwa, Karama and Deira. Dubai's large Indian and Pakistani expat community means there are plentiful affordable and delicious restaurants serving all manner of dishes from across the subcontinent. Dubai's Filipino contingent isn't quite as generously represented in culinary terms, but stroll around Satwa and you're likely to stumble across a number of innocuous restaurants serving simple, authentic and tasty Filipino fare.

Yet, for those who refuse to step through the threshold of anywhere other than a five-star hotel, there are still plenty of affordable options. Most, if not all of Dubai's hotel restaurants hold ongoing promotions – all-you-can-eat-deals – throughout the week to try and entice customers. Your best bet it to scour *Time Out's* weekly listings to discover the best current promotions around town. Then, there's the ubiquitous Dubai brunch…

Brunch

Despite the new-found maturity of Dubai's dining scene, there still remains a weekly institution that wonderfully encapsulates the essence of greedy indulgence: the brunch. What used to be a sophisticated halfway-house between breakfast and lunch has turned into a midday all-you-can-eat and all-you-can-drink dining extravaganza. 'Brunch' in its most modern incarnation is served everywhere from top five-star hotels and Irish bars to family-friendly restaurants, which charge a set price for luxury buffets, bottomless glasses, or a la carte deals for you to plough through each and every Friday. Yes, it's over the top and excessive, but you can't visit

Ravi's p123

An iftar feast

Dubai without having sampled at least one of the weekend brunches.

Ramadan

Since modern Dubai is all about consumption, it's fitting that a month of fasting is enforced by way of Ramadan, which usually falls around the month of August. During Ramadan's daylight hours, it's illegal to eat or drink (and smoke and chew gum) in public – a reason (combined with the searing summer temperatures) that induces many restaurants and bars to temporarily shut up shop until after the festival. But non-Muslims needn't fear – many will remain open, serving food behind closed doors (and curtains) until the breaking of the fast (iftar) at sunset. Like brunch, a traditional iftar feast is certainly worth experiencing (but for entirely different reasons). Not only does iftar feature piles of traditional dishes such as houmous, tabbouleh, kibbeh, friki, meats and spicy fish, but it is a fantastic community and family affair, and a valuable reminder of a local culture that

is too often lost amid the shining skyscrapers and sun loungers. Come Ramadan, all Dubai hotels will host variations of the iftar feast – often in buffet format, for a set price.

Bars & pubs

Though Dubai is technically a 'dry emirate', alcohol is permitted to be served and consumed on licensed premises – that is hotels and locations affiliated with hotels. Anywhere else in the world, drinking in a hotel bar would likely result in rubbing shoulders with depressed, lonely business travellers, but not so in Dubai – here, hotel bars are packed with residents and often endowed with splendid cityscape views, a beachside or poolside terrace, or are at least decorated in a vain attempt to resemble a traditional Irish pub (with varied degrees of success, we might add). Of course, the city's nationals won't be found propping up the bar, but this won't bother you too much when you're sipping poolside cocktails in the sun, gazing out over the Arabian Gulf.

Dubai Mall

Shopping

Dubai's shopping scene is probably its most lauded feature. Why? Well, all goods on offer are tax-free and there are sales – from luxury to market-stall bargains – everywhere you turn. Proof is in the construction: there are currently 68 functioning malls in the city and dozens more are planned to open in the next few years. Some of those in the pipeline, such as the proposed largest mall in the world, Mall of Arabia, have an at best uncertain, at worst doomed, chance of completion, but many of the smaller projects are still under way. (It's not as bad in Dubai as the international media would like to have you think – residents aren't all rolling around in dystopic, half-built landscapes, living in abandoned cars.)

Many tourists come to Dubai purely because it's a purchasing playground, particularly those from the rest of the GCC (Gulf Cooperation Council) and from Russia. While you'd be hard-pressed to visit the city without finding good shopping somewhere, the sheer volume can make the market hard to navigate.

Sales, sales, sales

When visiting Dubai solely (or at least partly) for shopping purposes, be strategic about the timing of your visit – you'll find sales running at almost any time of the year, but they certainly perk up during the government-sanctioned shopping 'festivals'. There's a month-long festival called Dubai Summer Surprises (that usually runs at some point between June and July – an unpleasantly hot time to visit) and there's also the Dubai Shopping Festival, the most impressive of the lot, which usually runs in January (when temperatures are mild). This month-long event sees the city overtaken by retail fever, with almost Dhs100 billion spent most years, as well as over Dhs1 billion worth of prizes on offer. Naturally, every year promises to be bigger than the last. This time of year also sees the opening of Global Village, a cheesy but charming outdoor market that is split into regions of the world. There are plenty of opportunities to find unusual crafts that you wouldn't find in malls, as well as a range of delicious food stalls (we love the Palestinian olive oil stand). For more on exact dates each year, visit www.mydsf.ae.

Mega malls

While *Time Out* tends to love the little boutiques around Dubai, there's no denying that the indie shopping scene can't compete with that in most major cities, including London, NYC or Sydney. However, when it comes to shopping centres so immense you can easily lose a family of 20 in them, Dubai knocks all other cities out of the park.

Since 2005, Dubai has had Mall of the Emirates (see p130), which at the time was the second largest mall in the Middle East, but has long since been overtaken. Home to the fascinating but carbon crazy Ski Dubai (see p136), this shopping complex sits snugly in the hearts of most long-term expats. Yes, newer malls have fancier car parking technology and higher ceilings, but MOE (to its friends) is still always busy. Also, last year, after realising that it was being usurped by the

S H O R T L I S T

Best independent store
- Bambah, Jumeirah (see p118)
- S*uce (see p119)
- THE One (see p119)

Best bookstore
- Book World by Kinokuniya, The Dubai Mall (see p105)

Best mall
- The Dubai Mall (see p105)
- Mall of the Emirates (see p131)

Best for regional design
- O'De Rose (see p138)

Best for electronics
- Carrefour, Mall of the Emirates (see p132)

Best for designer threads
- Boutique 1, The Walk, Dubai Marina (see p146)
- Symphony, The Dubai Mall (see p105)

Best for Arabic sweets
- Al Samadi Sweet Shop, The Boulevard, Old Town (see p102)

Best café for a rest
- Almaz by Momo, Mall of the Emirates (see p132)
- More, Dubai Mall (see p103)

Best cupcake store
- Magnolia Bakery, Bloomingdales, The Dubai Mall (see p104)

Best for shoes
- Manolo Blahnik, The Dubai Mall (see p105)

Best for buying gifts
- Gold Souk (see p65)

The fountains at Dubai Mall

newer kids on the Sheikh Zayed block, the Al Barsha mall opened a new extension – the Fashion Dome (see p132), which is home to high-end boutiques, as well as a range of food options that sit somewhere between food courts and high-end bistros (remember that many people in Dubai don't ever enter drinking establishments, so there are many mall eateries that feel like upmarket lounge bars).

All that said, mention mega malls and one name comes to mind in a blaze of neon lights: The Dubai Mall (see p105). The confidently named complex was completed in 2008 (making it about 15 years old in Dubai years, which are similar to those of a cat) and it is officially the largest mall in the world when it comes to total area. The shopping space spans 50 football fields – explaining why many people choose to use it as a space to improve their cardio in summer – and within its walls sit 22 cinema screens, 130 eateries (and counting) and over 1,000 shops. There are also plenty of attractions: an aquarium, an underwater zoo, an ice rink, the world's largest fountain (which, we're not going to lie to you readers, brings a tear to our eye), a theme park for kids, a theme park for

adults and a skate park. You can quite genuinely spend a whole day here – in fact, there's even a hotel, The Address Dubai Mall (see p168), so that you can enjoy a glass of wine mid-shop, if that's what you're after.

Two other malls that are worthy of honourable mentions are Dubai Festival Centre (see p77), which has its own mini-canal and marina, and Wafi (see p92) – the Egyptian-themed spot, good for luxury boutique shopping, licensed restaurants and olives (at Wafi Gourmet) (see p92).

Secret suburbs

While malls are the most concentrated shopping destinations in Dubai – there are no 'high streets' as such – but there are some parts of town that are also worth a gander, such as Satwa (see p124).

This is an older suburb with an authentic feel that is jam-packed with tailors, quirky haberdasheries, shoe menders and more. Stop at one of the many restaurants for some Filipino fare and then wander along the main drag Al Satwa Road, before hitting 'Plant Street' (see p124) which sells, you guessed it, plants, as well as randomly, art, old radios and calligraphic objects.

360°
Views

Discover the breathtaking sights along Dubai Creek onboard the elegant, air-conditioned and fully licensed Bateaux Dubai. Freshly prepared gourmet cuisine, panoramic views and personalised service make this a truly inspiring experience. Boarding starts at 7.45pm and Bateaux Dubai cruises at 8.30pm. Bateaux Dubai cruises every night for dinner and may be chartered for private events.

Location: Moored opposite the British Embassy in Bur Dubai, nearby Khalid Bin Waleed (Burjuman) metro station.

**For reservations please call +971 4 399 4994
or e-mail: mail@bateauxdubai.com**

www.bateauxdubai.com

bateaux dubai
A Unique Cruise Experience

Gold Souk

Further in the concrete jungle, Karama (see p87) is where you'll find Mark Fakobs handbags and Faulex watches, an experience that is worth trying once for the surreal experience of walking through fake offices and half floors (à la *Being John Malkovich*) to reach hidden rooms housing the shiniest new copies of your favourite it bags. There are also plenty of souvenir shop finds, bargains on comfy, velour tracksuits, high-end (and not) furniture stores and more.

The bustling beach community along JBR The Walk (see p146) feels like a love-child of the Middle East and holiday spots like the Gold Coast. While the sea and the many (mostly non-licensed) dining spots are the main pulling points, there are also quite a few boutiques and even a few galleries worth checking out. We particularly like the home design stores – Mood, Singways, Boutique 1 and Cottage Chic all deserve a mention.

Jumeirah (see p114) is the original suburb of most Dubai expats, and the main drag, Jumeirah Beach Road – which runs entirely parallel to the beach – is full of mini malls and well loved boutiques (most of which have been running for a decade or so and are well and truly Dubai institutions). In winter, it's worth parking up at one end and taking a stroll; however, in summer you'll want to take a taxi between the well air-conditioned mini malls.

Souk culture

While very few people who actually live in Dubai frequent the souks around town apart from when they're hosting visitors (bar the fruit and vegetable, and fish souks), a visit to the bustling older end of town is a must. While many malls like Souk Al Bahar (see p103) call themselves 'new souks', these bogus options have little to no atmosphere and it's the Creek-straddling suburbs of Deira and Bur Dubai that are home to the true-blue souks. The Gold Souk (see p65), with its near headache-inducing rows of shops stacked with blinding yellow gold, is unforgettable, as is the Spice Souk (see p65), where vendors will crack jokes with you. By contrast the Bastakiya market, set in the heritage buildings in Bur Dubai, will invite you to take in the beauty of traditional Arabian architecture. It also has a smattering of shops, art galleries and cafés.

Nasimi Beach

WHAT'S BEST
Nightlife

Like the city itself, Dubai's nightlife is a multicultural mish-mash of styles, music and people, full of contradictions and rich in variety. From Filipino cover bands thrashing out head-banging versions of 'Sweet Child O'Mine' in dingy dive bars, to 15,000 people sweating and bouncing in unison at a beach club on a man-made Palm-shaped island five kilometres into the middle of the Persian Gulf, you're never short of options.

Nightlife in Dubai is essentially split into two seasons: summer and not so summer. For eight months of the year, from the middle of October to the mid-point in May, open-air venues rule the sound waves and it's not hard to see why. With humidity low, night-time temperatures hovering around the 20s and the lighting supplied by the moon and stars, it's a winning combination that promoters and venues have been quick to seize on. Most clubs and venues come with an outdoor terrace, which is invariably the quickest to fill up, and thanks to open-air clubs like 360 and The Rooftop (see p139), Dubai can boast some of the best spaces in the world.

Considering the miles of pristine coastline, cooling breezes and year-round-sunshine, Dubai has been relatively slow to embrace beach clubs over the years, something that's been put right thanks to a sudden influx. Where before Barasti could justifiably claim to be the biggest, best and only beach club, it now competes with Nasimi, XL and a host of others all looking to sand and deliver. Sizzling all-day parties at these venues, usually running from 2pm-2am, dominate weekend clubbing and it's Nasimi – the beach club on the tip of the Palm – that's directed the scene for the last two years (see p155). Kitted out with a state-of-the-art Funktion 1 soundsystem, a quiet night for them constitutes 3,000 people, while mini-festivals like the biannual Sandance and the annual Chill Out festival routinely draw more than 10,000 clubbers.

But once June arrives, bringing with it rampant heat and humidity, clubbers move inside in search of AC, and the other side of Dubai's club scene gets to strut its stuff. With everything from high-end fashion clubs such as Cavalli (see p111) and Armani Privé (see p105) to three-room super-clubs like Trilogy (see p155), Chi (see p94) and Sanctuary (see p155), there's plenty on offer.

The other most notable change in Dubai's nightlife over the past decade has been its physical relocation. Where the Creek was once the business and social hub of Dubai, the city has since spread itself thickly along the coastline and the newly erected Marina – some 40km away from Old Dubai – is now home to thousands of expats who have made their nest in sky-scraping mega towers. While it might mean that Deira and its phalanx of dive bars are now less accessible, it has created dozens of venues in the new hotels that have sprung up across New Dubai. And where the hotels go, so too do the bars and clubs, as the sale of alcohol is restricted to hotels and, oddly enough, sports grounds.

As the entertainment heart of Dubai has progressed away from the old city, it's also raised the average drink prices. A bottle of

DON'T MISS

S H O R T L I S T

Best for alfresco
- 360, Jumeirah Beach Hotel (see p139)
- Nasimi Beach, Atlantis Hotel, The Palm (see p155)
- XL, Habtoor Grand (see p148)

Best for alternative music
- Casa Latina, Ibis Hotel, Al Barsha (see p135)
- The Music Room (see p88)
- Rock Bottom Cafe (see p88)

Best for a high-end club
- Cavalli Club, The Fairmont (see p111)
- Prive, Armani Hotel (see p105)

Best for clubbing
- Sanctuary, Atlantis Hotel (see p155)
- Trilogy, Madinat Jumeirah (see p139)

Best for bar food
- Dubai Marina Yacht Club (see p141)
- Loca, Dubai Marine Beach Resort (see p123)

Best for ladies' night
- Left Bank, Souk Al Bahar (see p106)
- Ultimate Ladies Night, Zinc (see p111)

Best cocktail bar
- Caramel, DIFC (see p97)
- Okku, The Monarch (see p108)
- Zuma, DIFC (see p100)

Best all-rounder
- Aquara Lounge, Dubai Marina Yacht Club (see p141)
- Barasti, Mina Seyahi Beach Resort & Spa (see p141)

beer is on average Dhs35, while you'll be lucky to get change from Dhs50 for a cocktail. Things escalate even further when you consider trying to sit down in any of the big name clubs. Table bookings are mandatory at most high-end clubs and come with a minimum spend, normally starting at Dhs1,500 for four people. That will get you a bottle of vodka, entry to the club and your waiter-serviced table. But if you splash out on a big bottle of champagne, some venues will serenade its arrival to your table with a quick blast of the *Star Wars* or *Superman* theme tune, and a sparkler display.

Those looking for a little more substance are well catered for in Dubai, but perhaps with not quite the same underground and alternative zeal as the UK. Big bands regularly make a stop-off in Abu Dhabi to play at the impressive Yas Island complex 40 minutes away from Dubai, with Guns N'

Roses, Stevie Wonder and Snoop Dogg all recent visitors. Not to be outdone, Dubai also hosts a variety of big international stars, recently including Moby and Maroon 5, but as with the alcohol prices, you'll pay for the privilege – most tickets start from Dhs200 and can go up to Dhs750, depending on whether you want to be a VIP or VVIP. The city is also blessed with some of the best DJ talent on a regular basis. Big names like Tiesto and Armin Van Buuren are frequent guests, while clubs like Trilogy, 360, Chi and Sanctuary have welcomed everyone from Mark Ronson to Frankie Knuckles to their decks. Hip hop and house heads are well catered for, and while the alternative scene can be a little sporadic, there are regular indie/drum and bass/funk and soul nights to keep you dancing. Most clubs charge anywhere from Dhs50-Dhs100 for regular nights, and up to Dhs200 for special one-off events. Ladies can sometimes get in

Stevie Wonder at Yas Island

OASIS WITH AN
URBAN TWIST

Allow us to redefine your perception of luxury as you are welcomed to a hotel filled with surprises. Our philosophy ensures that convention is forever challenged to deliver excellence beyond the expected. Explore Meliá Dubai and discover an urban oasis in bustling Bur Dubai.

MELIÃ
DUBAI

Opening Fall 2011

you are the journey

melia.com
melia-dubai.com

for free and couples are often given preferred treatment in the queues, while groups of men might have to stand out in the heat for longer.

Due to red tape and prohibitive licensing restrictions, putting on live music is a costly venture, so aside from the large-scale events, there aren't many avenues for budding bands (not to mention the fact you need to be 21 or over to legally enter a licensed venue in the first place). Live music bars and clubs have countered this by employing cover bands to hammer out the pop, rock and hip hop hits, seven nights a week. Some, notably the Rock Spiders, have built up a cult-following, while others fall into the slightly-better-than-a-CD category.

Outside of the vibrant club and music scene, Dubai has plenty to offer. The Laughter Factory is a popular alternative, hosting three comedians on a seven-stop monthly tour across Dubai and Abu Dhabi. Theatre has yet to fully take off in Dubai, but the Madinat and DUCTAC at Mall of the Emirates both have well put together programmes and regularly sell out their plays and productions. Elsewhere, big companies like Cirque du Soleil are rumoured to be setting up a semi-permanent base in the emirate, while the city has been inundated by late-night dining and lounge bars, with upscale chains like Nobu, Mahiki and Zuma opening predictably expensive but chic locations that mix a club-like atmosphere with top quality food and drinks.

It's worth bearing in mind that while Dubai might be the most liberal extension of the Middle East, it's still a Muslim country, and therefore certain behaviour is not tolerated. Drinking is not allowed in public places and you'll need an alcohol licence via one of the two distributors if you want to buy

booze in the city (although you can purchase alcohol at the airport's duty free). You'll also be expected to dress appropriately. Daytime bikinis and swimming shorts are fine at beach parties, but come sundown, you'll be asked to cover up. Most clubs won't allow you in with flip flops, shorts or baseball caps, even though they might be essential items in deep summer.

Dubai follows a Friday-Saturday weekend, so the fun starts on Thursday evening and ends on Saturday night, which can take some getting used to. Sunday and Monday are generally quiet nights, although you can find some good deals around, and Tuesdays are commonly known as ladies' night across the city. Women can drink for free in many of the bars around town, while men have to pay the normal prices.

Most pubs and bars will open from 6pm and have licences until 3am, with happy hours common between 6pm-8pm. Clubs generally run from 10pm-3am, although you'll often find that most don't fill up until midnight, and sometimes even later. The legal drinking age is 21 across the UAE and most venues enforce this rigidly, so don't be upset if you're asked for ID at the door. Some venues will only accept passports as ID, so bring a copy of your passport with you if you can.

All drinks are subject to a 10 per cent service charge, but as this normally goes straight to the hotel rather than the bar staff, leave a cash tip of 10 per cent if it's warranted. Unlike some of Europe, Dubai is a smoker's paradise: packets cost around Dhs7 in the shops (double that if you buy them behind the bar). Smoking in bars and clubs is still legal in Dubai, but with many having outdoor terraces, you shouldn't have to go far to find a smoke-free atmosphere.

The Pavilion

Arts & Leisure

Dubai, as many people are aware, is a city of opposites. On the one hand you have decadence, luxury and big boys' toys, in the form of jet skis, yachts or million-dollar waterparks, and on the other you have a haven for Middle Eastern art, showcasing hard-hitting subjects like abuse, neglect, political grievance and regional identity.

Art scene

Dubai is a liberal refuge for art in the Middle East and artists from Libya, Saudi Arabia and Iran flock to the city to showcase their political and controversial views through intricate mediums that are interpreted, but never defined, to avoid censorship issues. This year,

more projects have emerged that go against the grain of the more obvious bling-style culture that you'll see driving around in souped up 4x4s. Recently, the arts got a further boost with the opening of The Pavilion (see p106) – a modern Swedish-style minimalist space that would look more at home in Hoxton than in Dubai. The long-overdue venue is buzzing with black-rimmed spectacle types, who while away the hours sipping coffee and perusing their Apple laptops and exhibitions in its chic white spaces. The gallery is also keen to promote film nights and community events.

While Dubai still has no real art museum to speak of and some galleries have closed because of the financial crisis, cluster areas, such as in the Al Quoz industrial area and the DIFC, still gently bubble away. Down in the heritage Bastakiya district you'll find more traditional, smaller art galleries, which predominantly feature Middle Eastern art and Arabic calligraphy.

What hasn't been affected by the recession is the local appetite for collecting both contemporary and old, regional and global, art at auction. Sotheby's, Christie's and Bonham's all have very active offices in Dubai; 2010 saw a 117 per cent rise in profits for one auction house and records are constantly being broken, especially at painting and jewellery sales.

Me time

Dubai doesn't mess about when it comes to pampering and it doesn't take long for people new to the city to get into the swing of being regularly massaged, waxed, kneaded and beautified. For both women and men, the options are endless, with each five-star hotel in town fielding an impressive spa and pool, plus extras like saunas, steam rooms and Jacuzzis. If you need relaxing and can't spend a fortune, then the city's well catered for, with local brands offering budget massages and beauty treatments, usually for around Dhs250. Salons have also started popping up in malls – Nivea Haus offers a huge range of treatments for girls and guys in The Dubai Mall, while Spaces in the Iconic store in Deira City Centre is the place to pop to for a mid-shopping manicure.

A favourite way to spend a weekend in Dubai (especially in the blistering summer) is to indulge in a spa day – a package of one or two treatments, which then gets you access to the hotel's facilities for the day. In the winter, hotels also offer up beach or pool access by the day,

S H O R T L I S T

Best for Arabic art
- Farjam Gallery (see p100)
- Majlis Gallery (see p89)

Best for photography
- Empty Quarter gallery (see p100)

Best for modern art
- Traffic gallery (see p113)
- XVA gallery (see p102)

Best for a play
- DUCTAC (see p135)

Best for a barbeque
- Jumeirah Beach Park (see p121)
- Safa Park (see p112)

Best water experience
- Swimming with dolphins, Atlantis, Palm Jumeirah (see p155)
- Swimming with sharks, Underwater Zoo, The Dubai Mall (see p106)

Best for winter sports
- Ice Rink, The Dubai Mall (see p106)
- Ski Dubai, Mall of Emirates (see p135)

Best spa
- Amara Spa, Park Hyatt (see p71)
- Talise Spa, Jumeirah Emirates Towers (see p100)

Best infinity pool
- The Address Downtown (see p168)
- The Address Dubai Marina (see p173)

Best for sundowners
- Bahri Bar, Madinat Jumeriah (see p136)

It's all in the experience

With 23 years of experience and a host of accolades, Dubai Golf's championship golf courses at Emirates Golf Club and the Dubai Creek Golf & Yacht Club have garnered unparalleled prestige. So whether you're taking a swing where the world's top golfers have played or enjoying our award-winning hospitality, you're guaranteed an experience that has become internationally renowned.

To book your tee time please call +971 4 380 1234
or email golfbooking@dubaigolf.com

dubaigolf.com

so visitors can make the move from a public, free beach to one serviced by people bringing you cool towels and ice cold water.

Time off

Dubai is a work hard, play hard city – residents go all out to make the most of their leisure time and Dubai's not short of things to do. Indoor sports exist aplenty here, all in air-conditioned comfort – from bowling at Al Nasr Leisureland (see p95) to zipping downhill at the infamous Ski Dubai (see p135), the region's only indoor ski slope. In the last couple of years, a new ice rink has opened at The Dubai Mall (see p106), and you can now go flying with an indoor skydiving centre at the out-of-town Mirdif City Centre.

Dubai and the surrounding areas are also perfect for indulging in some extreme sports. Although not as 'on the map' as other extreme sports destinations like New Zealand, Dubai's landscape is perfect for a range of activities. This means uncrowded facilities and seas perfect for surfing, wakeboarding, kiteboarding and diving.

For a once in a lifetime experience, head to Skydive Dubai (see p151) and jump out of a plane 13,000 feet above the Palm Jumeirah – one of the only times (unless you spot it from a commerical flight) you'll see its actual shape. For those that prefer to be in the sea rather than hurtling towards it, Dubai offers decent, consistent swell most year round, with the best waves around what is known locally as Sunset Beach (next to the Burj Al Arab). In the last few years, a large surfing community has sprung up around the surf school and shop, (www.surfschooluae.com). Next to them on the beach, you'll find a huge number of kiteboarders – their enormous colourful wings can be seen for miles along the beach.

Out of town, the desert plays host to a range of adrenaline-based activities, from sand-boarding to quad biking, dune bashing and more. The best way to experience these is to book with a local tour operator, such as Arabian Adventures (www.arabian-adventures.com). Hidden in the depths of the Gulf is an abundance of marine life, including turtles

Ski Dubai

Diving in Musandam

and white-tip reef sharks, spotted daily off the coast of Fujairah. Keen divers and snorkellers can head over to the east coast of the UAE for diving excursions around wrecks, or book on to a dhow boat cruise around Musandam to spot the friendly local dolphins.

Beaches

And if all that sounds like too much hard work, why not simply hit the beach? Although private developments have carved up the seafront, there are still public beaches. Russian Beach in Jumeirah 1, Sunset Beach near the Burj Al Arab and Jumeirah Beach Residence (JBR) beach at Dubai Marina are all public spaces – but come prepared. Unlike other cities, there are no facilities to buy water or snacks, and little shade. For a more pleasant experience, head to Jumeirah Beach Park on Jumeirah Beach Road (see p121). It costs Dhs3 per person and the park runs down on to the sand, has barbecue areas, plenty of palm trees for shade and a small café selling drinks, snacks and ice creams. Remember, however, you might be on the beach in your

bikini or boardshorts but Dubai is still a conservative country: you'll need to cover up when you leave, since wandering round malls or supermarkets in your swimwear won't be appreciated and could get you into trouble.

Theatre

While not as comprehensive as Dubai's commitment to extreme sports, there is a small theatre scene in Dubai. The Madinat Theatre (see p139) plays host to many international productions – recent shows have included *Mamma Mia!* and *Hairspray,* and while the runs are nowhere near as long as in other cities, the increased frequency of big-budget productions suggests that enjoying a night at the theatre is becoming more feasible. For the less mainstream numbers, check out Dubai Community Theatre and Arts Centre (DUCTAC) at Mall of the Emirates (see p135), which plays host to offbeat plays from international and regional artists. The multi-functional centre has interesting exhibitions in its Gallery of Light space and holds regular workshops for artists.

Calendar

Omega Dubai Desert Golf Classic

What follows is a list of the best events in Dubai, from those that had been announced at the time of press. For up-to-the-minute event details, pick up a copy of *Time Out Dubai* magazine or go to www.timeoutdubai.com. Most of these events take place annually, but dates for future years were unavailable at the time of going to press, so check the website for details on dates and prices. Approximate dates have been given for public holidays, as these are dependent on the sighting of the moon, and appear in bold.

January

Early Jan **International Parachuting Championships & Gulf Cup**
Skydive Dubai, Dubai Marina
www.skydivedubai.ae
Is it a bird? Is it a plane? No, it's the world's best stunt parachutists and skydivers, who have dropped in on Dubai for the last two years. Head down to The Walk for a decent view of the action.

Mid Jan **Dubai Shopping Festival**
Various locations
www.mydsf.com
Dubai celebrates what it does best, with this annual month-long discount bonanza. Go crazy on the retail therapy and watch out for up to Dhs1 billion worth of giveaways in the malls and fireworks over Dubai Creek every night.

Late Jan **Standard Chartered Dubai Marathon**
Jumeirah Beach Road
www.premiermarathons.com
Runners beat the heat with an early start, as they pace the length of Dubai's Beach Road and back to the marina, to clock up those kilometres. A fun-run and a 10-kilometre run also happen on the same day.

February

Ongoing Dubai Shopping Festival (see January)

Early Feb **Omega Dubai Desert Golf Classic**
Emirates Golf Club
www.dubaidesertclassic.com
Watch some of the finest on the fairways strut their stuff. Spaniard Alvaro Quiros won it in 2011.

15-17 **Skywards Dubai International Jazz Festival**
Dubai Media City Amphitheatre
www.dubaijazzfest.com
The annual 'jazz' festival tends to lean towards more mainstream musicians and bands for the headline slots. David Gray, Macy Gray and Jamie Cullum have all performed in previous years.

Mid Feb Mouloud (Birth of the Prophet)

Late Feb-early March **Dubai Duty Free Tennis Championships**
Tennis Stadium, Garhoud
www.atpworldtour.com
The top seeds in the world battle it out over a week in Garhoud, as part of the ATP World Tour, for prize money of over a million dollars.

March

Early March **Emirates Airline International Festival of Literature**
Various locations
www.eaifl.com
Dubai's literary festival regularly attracts big name authors like Michael Palin, as well as a range of Middle Eastern writers.

Mid March **Dubai International Boat Show**
Dubai International Marine Club
www.boatshowdubai.com
Go to gawp at the seriously luxurious floating palaces up for grabs, as lucrative buyers flood into Dubai to snap up the latest line of superyachts.

Mid March **Dubai International Arabian Horse Championship**
Dubai International Convention and Exhibition Centre
www.diahc.ae
Arabian horses are huge business within the region and the most prized are put through their paces here, in this show designed to rank their beauty, agility and heritage.

Mid March **RAK Half Marathon**
www.rakmarathon.org
Possibly the richest half marathon in the world, athletes descend

Skywards Dubai International Jazz Festival

Dubai World Cup

on the sleepy emirate of Ras Al Khaimah and hit the road running.

Mid March **Taste of Dubai**
Dubai Media City Amphitheatre
www.tasteofdubaifestival.com
This annual foodie fair has grown massively in size over the last two years to include workshops, a gourmet market, masterclasses and of course, all the restaurants' sample stands. UK chefs James Martin and Gary Rhodes tend to pop up here year on year.

Mid March **Art Week**
Various locations
www.artdubai.ae
Having started off as a simple art fair (Art Dubai), the confusingly named Art Week now runs over most of the month. From high-end art collector parties to open-top bus gallery tours, it also includes events in Sharjah and Abu Dhabi.

Mid March-early April **Dubai World Cup**
Meydan Racecourse
www.duabiworldcupdcom
The richest horse race in the world is celebrated in town with Dubai's version of Ascot. It's as much about the hats as it is about the horses.

April

Ongoing **Dubai World Cup**
(see March)

Early April **The Bride Show**
Dubai International Convention & Exhibition Centre
www.thebrideshow.com/dubai
A month-long extravaganza which celebrates everything wedding-based. The exhibition includes demonstrations and fashion shows, as well as shopping opportunities.

Early April **Chill Out Festival**
Nasimi Beach, Atlantis,
The Palm Jumeirah
www.chilloutfestivaldubai.com
A two-day musical extravaganza that brings more leftfield and world music to Dubai's shores than the regular clubs would normally allow to grace the decks. Hot Chip, Röyksopp and Matthew Herbert all gently rocked 2011.

Late April **Gulf Film Festival**
Various venues
www.gulffilmfest.com
Now in its fourth year, this festival aims to broaden local film horizons as well as provide a platform for local filmmakers.

VERO MODA®

May

Early May **Photo World Dubai**
www.photoworld-dubai.com
A digital and image exhibition that's also open to the public. Check the website for details on workshops.

June

Late June **Summer in Dubai**
Various locations
www.dubaievents.ae
The shopping festival previously known as Dubai Summer Surprises is now promoted as Summer in Dubai. The malls make the most of the air conditioning they offer and host a range of discounts, activities and events with families in mind. Check the website for details on giveaways and competitions which get bigger and better each year.

**Late June Leilat al-Meiraj
(Ascension of the Prophet)**

July

Ongoing **Summer in Dubai**
(see June)

Late July **Ramadan**
The Muslim holy month depends on the lunar calendar but will start in late July in 2012. In public, no smoking, eating, drinking or chewing gum is allowed between sunrise and sunset, while a more modest dress sense should be adhered to.

August

Mid August **HopFest**
Irish Village
www.irishvillage.ae
The popular annual beer-drinking festival provides a couple of days' respite from the heat in an air-conditioned marquee. Over 120 beers from around the world are shipped in and the buffet table is on permanent stand-by.

The Bride Show p41

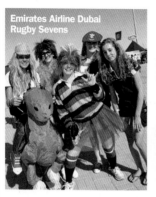

Emirates Airline Dubai Rugby Sevens

Late August Eid Al Fatr

Ramadan is broken with the public national holiday, Eid Al Fatr. As with Ramadan, dates are only officially announced a few days before, based on the sighting of the new moon.

October

Mid Oct **Gulf Bike Week**

Half Hells Angels love-in, half music festival, the sound of thousands of Harleys can be heard throughout this week. On the music side of things, Amy Winehouse and Pharrell Williams headlined in 2011, while a bike show celebrated everything on two wheels, from the humble BMX upwards.

Mid Oct **Oktoberfest**

Irish Village, Garhoud

It doesn't matter that Germany is nearly six hours away, Dubai celebrates this beer-guzzling festival with its usual relish. German ales and delicacies are on offer as well as live local music.

November

Early Nov Eid al-Adha (Feast of the Sacrifice)

Late Nov Al-Hijra (Islamic New Year)

December

2 National Day

Dubai celebrates the birth of the United Arab Emirates as one unfied country, which saw the emirates of Ajman, Abu Dhabi, Fujairah, Dubai, Sharjah, Ras Al Khaimah and Umm Al Quwain come together in 1971. Watch out for plenty of fireworks, festivities and special offers.

Early Dec **Emirates Airline Dubai Rugby Sevens**

The Sevens Stadium

www.dubairugby7s.com

Whether you love rugby or not, the Sevens is one of the biggest three-day parties of the year. Expats go wild in the aisles of the stadium, with fancy dress outfits, sing-alongs and plenty of good-natured team rivalry. A proper experience.

Early Dec **Dubai International Film Festival**

Various venues

www.dubaifilmfest.com

Dubai's annual stab at a film festival attracts international stars and Hollywood A-listers, with a mix of mainstream premieres and plenty of Middle Eastern highlights. There are workshops for anyone in the business.

Capital music

For stadium-selling artists, head to Abu Dhabi.

Yas Hotel

Since the hotly anticipated opening of the Formula One Grand Prix circuit in 2009, Abu Dhabi's Yas Island has become one of the most-played venues in the UAE for visiting megastars, from Aerosmith to Beyoncé, Snoop Dogg to Stevie Wonder. A short drive from Dubai, Yas Island pitches itself as a fully-functioning leisure destination all on its own, and not just an extension of Formula One frolics. It houses a five-star hotel (of course) and the world's first Ferrari World theme park alongside its track and concert arena. Yas Hotel, which straddles part of the racing circuit, is home to one of Abu Dhabi's most prolific nightclubs, Allure, as well as numerous restaurants and suites overlooking the track. There's also the Yas Links Golf Course, while the island's marina is home to the Abu Dhabi branch of Monaco's famous Stars 'N' Bars eaterie as well.

Yas Island's Show Weekends are fast becoming a meaty presence on the annual calendar, with acts such as Shakira, Tiesto and Kanye West all putting on well-attended sets, along with day-long events like Creamfields, which, for the record, is a far cry in more ways than one from the original. The weekends don't follow a set pattern; performers are announced last minute as one-off concerts. Check www.timeoutdubai.com for up-to-date announcements.

Over on Saadiyat Island, there's not much worth writing home about – yet. The island is anticipated to become a cultural hub in the region, home to a Guggenheim Museum, a Louvre (complete with priceless works of art on loan from Paris) and a performing arts centre designed by renowned Arabic architect Zaha Hadid. And as it's the UAE, you can bet your bottom dollar that in the end, there'll be shops and restaurants to boot.

Located on the bustling district of The Walk, the 5 star Mövenpick Hotel Jumeirah Beach blends cosmopolitan lifestyle and relaxation. This fashionable retreat features lively dining and entertainment choices, expansive recreational and modern meeting facilities... just few steps from the stunning blue waters of the Arabian Gulf.

Passionately Swiss.™

MÖVENPICK
Hotel Jumeirah Beach

Mövenpick Hotel Jumeirah Beach
P.O. Box 282825, Dubai, United Arab Emirates
Phone +971 4 449 8888, Fax +971 4 449 8889
hotel.jumeirahbeach@moevenpick.com

www.moevenpick-hotels.com

Dip in ✚ chill out.

Itineraries

Bastakiya

Down on the Water

The casual observer would be forgiven for thinking that it is impossible to walk anywhere in Dubai. From airport to beachside hotel, it looks like a series of giant, unforgiving flumes of concrete. And it's true that this is not a city that is kind to pedestrians; most of its roads are big highways more suited to Hummers and cargo trucks than inquisitive walkers.

The Creek, at the heart of what Dubai was before the oil, is a plodder's paradise. It has shaded alleys and curious crannies, and takes just a couple of hours to explore. Start at 2pm and you'll be finishing around sunset. The best place to begin is the **Dubai Museum** (see p81). It's small and can be a little cramped, but it's the only place that offers a historical view of the city. The introductory video near the entrance runs like an excitable promotional blurb for

Dubai, but does have a few unique, old images. The large boards around this room show the growth of the city through the 20th century. Other rooms have exhibits on pearl diving, dhow building, nomadic life and local flora and fauna. The simple explanations of life before Dubai's hyperdevelopment (particularly the harshness of a pearl diver's existence) can be fascinating. The museum is on a roundabout just outside the **Bastakiya** area (see p81). As you exit, turn left and head along Al Fahidi Street. Before you reach the next roundabout, turn left into one of the alleys next to the Sheikh Mohammed Centre for Cultural Understanding. You are now in Bastikiya. Iranian traders settled in this district more than a century ago and built homes out of coral, topped with wind towers that served as natural air conditioning units. Today, the wind towers are merely decorative, but in the past, Dubai's citizens hung wet cloths in them when the summer was especially cruel. These would cool the air before it entered the home, giving inhabitants some much needed respite from the heat. Aside from the towers, this neighbourhood is home to some of the city's smaller independent galleries and a few quaint outdoor cafés.

Start at the **Majlis Gallery** (see p89), just off Al Fahidi Street. It houses a wonderful collection of local art, including paintings, illustrations, sculpture, silverwork and Arabian trinkets. You can browse the entire collection in half an hour and leave anything you buy with the owners to collect later. Step out of Majlis, turn right, and a few metres down you'll see the **Basta Art Café** (see p89), a beautiful courtyard eatery. After looking at their limited range of local crafts, get a table in the shade of the central tree and order some super-healthy

Arabian wraps or salads, washed down with mint and lime juice.

Once you're refreshed, continue the heritage walk by turning right down the narrow alleyway that separates the Majlis Gallery and Basta Art Café. At the end of the alley, you'll see the back of the **XVA Gallery** (see p86), an idyllic slice of old Arabia, hung with white fabric and home to regular exhibitions. It also has a hotel upstairs, with a few cute, atmospheric rooms. Climb up to the roof and you'll get a view over the area's wind towers, minarets and cobbled streets. Take in the art and the local jewellery, clothing and magazines in the store before stopping for a drink in the courtyard. Leaving XVA, head out of the wind tower quarter and down towards the Creek. You'll emerge next to the Bastakiya Mosque, near a clutch of abras for hire. Walk past these as far as you can and turn left into the **Textile Souk** (see p87).

Majlis Gallery

Can't have enough of it.

Whether it's a casual stroll in the snow park throwing snow balls with your kids, a leisurely ride in the ski lift or a cup of piping hot chocolate in the Avalanche café on the slope, there's so much more to SkiDubai than skiing.

If you haven't been here before, you've been missing out on the time of your life. **Be warned though, it's addictive.**

SKI DUBAI
سكي دبي

been there yet?

Abra Station

The wares on offer are firmly aimed at tourists, so anyone after a genuine bargain on fabrics would do better to head to Satwa. Weave through this network of cloth-pushing salesmen and you'll rejoin the Creek. You may find that abra skippers will approach you and offer tours for anything up to Dhs100. Politely decline and head for the **Bur Dubai Abra Station** (see p80) directly in front of where you stand. You'll be hustled on with everyone else and pay just Dhs1 for the five minute journey to Deira.

These water taxis chug back and forth, ferrying a quarter of a million people a month across the Creek, and are a vital means of transport for the city's low-paid workers. Though today there's competition from super-sleek luxury yachts and the city's water taxis, tourists still seem to love the old-fashioned

abras. As your abra barges its way into the Sabkha Abra Station on the other side, you'll notice the battered old dhows to your left. These come from Iran and across the Gulf, packed high with spices, toys, TVs and household goods, which are then stacked by the side of the road for collection. The dhows also serve as housing for the crew and a stroll along the wharf gives a sneak peak into a sailor's life.

Opposite the abra station, a narrow road runs into the Old Souk. As you enter, the first few stalls to the left sell fairly generic tourist trinkets – wooden camels, glowing Burj Al Arabs and the like – but just past these, to the right, is the more scenic **Spice Souk** (see p65). The name sounds grander than the reality, but this run of eight or nine shops down one cramped street is atmospheric

Sinéquanone

and smells wonderful. You can buy saffron here for a relatively cheap price. Push on up the main drag, passing more souvenir stalls and touts selling 'copy watches' and fake Louis Vuitton, until you reach the cornea-troubling sparkler that is the **Gold Souk** (see p65). Prices here are fixed according to the day's gold price per gram, with an extra charge for workmanship. The more intricate the piece, the more you have to pay – and if you are buying, haggle heartily and be prepared to look as though you're moving on… chances are the price will suddenly come down. If you're just there for a look, 20 minutes of strolling through the alleys is usually enough.

Then, retrace your steps and take an abra back to Bur Dubai. As you disembark, turn right and walk around the Creek. It's a 10-minute saunter to Al Shindagha, the other remaining pocket of the original old town of Dubai, where you can take a trip around Sheikh Saeed's childhood home. **The Heritage Village and Diving Village** (see p84) are also here, but displays can be uninspiring. Sometimes Bedouins set up camp in the former, complete with camels and open fires. At other times, it's just a desolate bit of scrubland with a few shops selling tourist tat. If they're around, the Emirati women selling fried dough balls covered in date syrup are worth a visit. And once the strolling is all done, head to the terrace of one of the Arabian restaurants nearby for a shisha, mezze and lashings of mint tea as you watch the sun set over the Creek.

ITINERARIES

Spice Souk p51

Ibn Battuta Mall

Metro Malls

In the past, the only excuse you had for not spending an entire day at the shopping malls around town was because it was tiresome driving around, but not anymore. With the opening of the Dubai Metro in 2009, it's as easy as hopping on and off a train. Where else but Dubai can you spend an entire day in air-conditioned comfort, despite the searing heat? And, as anyone who's been here long enough will tell you, malls in Dubai are for far more than just a spot of retail therapy.

Start your day at Ibn Battuta Mall, the world's largest themed shopping mall, designed to reflect the journeys of Ibn Battuta, the 14th-century Arab explorer who set off to travel the world at the wise old age of 20. Have a delicious, healthy breakfast at Lime Tree Café, tucked away in a courtyard, before exploring the world as Ibn Battuta did. Each region that he went to –

Andalusia, Tunisia, Egypt, Persia, India and China – is reflected in the decor of the six 'courts' of the mall. You will find a life-size elephant, a huge boat, gorgeous mosaics and plenty of exhibits that will give you an insight into the history and global influence of the Arab world. There are many high-street and boutique stores here, from New Look and River Island to Ginger & Lace, Betsey Johnson and Bauhaus. But even if you don't want to shop, check out what's playing at the city's only **IMAX screen** (see p149), where movies come supersized on a 44ft-tall, 70ft-wide screen, complete with surround sound and often in 3D.

While at Ibn Battuta, don't forget to book yourself a ride on the big yellow balloon. Sky Dubai Adventure gives you the chance to ride the world's largest (of course) helium, tethered balloon, which takes off every 15 minutes to give you 360-degree views of 'new Dubai' from 150m high (04 363 6552).

Next, head down the Dubai Metro Red line and get off at **Mall of the Emirates** (see p130) – the only mall with an indoor ski resort. How often is it possible to ski on snow in the desert? **Ski Dubai** (see p136) lets you have a run down the slope if you think you know what you're doing, but also conducts regular lessons in the dome (for every training level). If you think one plank is better than two, you can have a go with the snowboarders too. The snow park is a favourite with little ones – you'll see them whizzing along the tobogganing hills, tubing or enjoying a bobsled ride. Oh, and fun in the transparent dome is on display to all of the mall shoppers, so keep your best frozen smile on. Have lunch at stylish **Aprés** (see p127) that has some of the best views of the ski slope and where, unusually for a mall restaurant in Dubai, you can order a glass of wine with your meal. Afterwards, head to Harvey Nichols (see p132), for some window shopping or visit the new Fashion Dome where you'll find plenty of high-end fashion stores, including Diane Von Furstenberg, Christian Louboutin and Dolce & Gabbana.

Mall of the Emirates

ITINERARIES

The Dubai Mall

When you've had enough, walk back to the metro station and continue along the Red line, getting off at the Burj Khalifa Station, where you'll find **The Dubai Mall** (see p105). Yes, it's got a 'world's biggest' tag too, but it deserves it. This behemoth mall has it all, from the **Dubai Fountains** (see p102), a choreographed fountain show designed by the same creators of the those at Bellagio in Las Vegas, to the world's tallest tower, **Burj Khalifa** (see p102), right on its doorstep. The mall is a destination like no other, so kick off the tour with a coffee at local chain More, on the mall's waterfront promenade, to watch the dancing jets of water (just as entertaining is watching the crowd 'ahhing' at the fountain), before stepping into the only **Bloomingdale's** store (see p104) outside the US. This 146,000-sq-ft, three-level store is unlike anything you'll have ever seen before. On the lower ground level you'll find the homewares department, which is chock-a-block with quirky goods and Magnolia Bakery, the iconic cupcake store made famous by the *Sex in the City* series – yum! Move up to the main part of the mall and you'll find the stunningly designed beauty section (complete with black and white-tiled floor), the oh-so expensive clothes department, as well as the more affordable, younger fashion area.

Take a break from shopping to go swimming with the sharks. **The Underwater Zoo** (see p106) at The Dubai Mall is home to 33,000 animals (yes, feeding time is always fun here) and kids and adults will both love the walk-through tunnel that lets visitors get a closer look at their favourite fish. If you're feeling brave, the best thing to do is jump right into this unique PADI dive site and swim with scaries, such as sand tiger sharks and stingrays, with dives and snorkeling organised by Al Boom Diving. If you're the

Deira City Centre

type who likes to keep adrenaline levels well and truly muted, give the sharks a miss and instead watch an arthouse flick at **The Picturehouse** (see p106) that is located inside the extensive Reel Cinemas complex here. Dubai's only artsy cinema plays foreign films, interesting documentaries and anything that's not a 'blockbuster'.

Before the evening, get back on the metro towards the City Centre Metro Station to reach **Deira City Centre** (see p70) only a few stops away, for some serious high-street shopping. Name the brand and you'll find it here – Bershka, Forever 21, H&M, Mango, Monsoon, Promod, Stradivarius, Topshop and even a Warehouse. You can easily pick up a few tops and trousers for less than Dhs1,000 at each store, but make sure you stop by the 2,000-sq-ft **Iconic** store (see p71) for some serious retail pleasure. Not only does it have quirky (and affordable) fashion and an extensive beauty

section packed with cosmetics, perfumes and the best bath and body products in the market, but there's a spa and salon in-store too, along with two restaurants and a section devoted entirely to electronics. You'll especially love the kitschy Soho collection that includes random items such as stationery, funky household pieces and even a few interesting books.

You'll no doubt be tired of holding all those shopping bags, so for the last time, hop back on the Metro and get back to **The Dubai Mall** (see p105) for an unforgettable dinner at **At.mosphere**, the tallest restaurant in the world (see p103). Located on the 122nd floor of the Burj Khalifa, this international bar, restaurant and grill offers diners an unforgettable view with their five-star meal. At around 800 metres above sea level, you can watch the sun set over the entire city and gaze out to sea at the picturesque Arabian Gulf.

Living the New Life

The party never ends in New Dubai. From signature meals at beach lounges to the hottest bars and superstar DJs playing at packed clubs in town, the city proves that all that's glitzy is indeed gold. There's so much to see and do in the (relatively new) neighbourhoods of Palm Jumeirah and Dubai Marina. While there's a fair bit of family fun to be had at hotel beach clubs and the shopping malls in the area, these iconic districts always draw the bold and the beautiful after dark.

To experience the best New Dubai has to offer, start with lunch at **West 14th** (see p154) at Oceana Beach Club in Palm Jumeirah. Even though some parts of the Palm seem to forever be under construction, it provides a great setting for a steakhouse – the first-frond location affords fabulous views of Dubai's coastline and it is conveniently situated next to the resort's outdoor

bar. Inside, guests are left in no doubt as to the restaurant's theme – faux exposed-brick walls, dark reds, low lighting and exposed pipes running across the ceiling will all transport you from Dubai to NYC's Meatpacking District. The dining experience is enhanced by thoughtful touches, such as the different steak knives and mustard trolley, but it's the prime cuts of meat that will always be the star attraction. Tender, delicious and cooked to perfection.

Afterwards, grab a taxi and head to **101** (see p151) at the One&Only The Palm. The views served up at this lounge are the perfect excuse to enjoy a few post-meal drinks while you soak in the St.Tropez-esque vibe. 101's al fresco seating opens onto a fashionable chillout lounge with seaside tables and a bar. It's a good choice during the cooler months, but if you're keen to move on, it's time to hop on a boat. Yes, a boat. The resort actually has its own private marina and if you reserve in advance, a ferry service will see you glide across the waters of the Arabian Gulf from The Palm to its sister property, the **One&Only Royal Mirage** (see p173) at Al Sufouh, just a short taxi drive away from the Dubai Marina district. High on the list of top attractions here is the **Dubai Marina Yacht Club** (see p141), one of the largest private yacht clubs in the world, with a purpose-built clubhouse and four marinas spread over a man-made 3.5 kilometre canal. It includes fine dining restaurants, lounges, a cigar and billiards room and a fully licensed bar area, so you won't be short of things to indulge in, apart from gazing lustily at the multi-million dollar floating palaces. Also, towards the end of the year, the club hosts an annual Dragon Boat Festival that sees many community groups, not just in Dubai but across

the country, put their best stroke forward and compete.

For sundowners, however, you can't beat **Barasti** at Le Méridien Mina Seyahi Beach Resort & Marina (see p141). This *Time Out* award-winning beach bar has been around for more than a decade and the popularity of the decked, sun-drenched venue shows no signs of waning. Many people choose to head to the new kid on the block – **Nasimi** at Atlantis, Palm Jumeirah – which is good too (especially in winter). But what you'll like about Barasti is that the crowd reflects the different strands of Dubai's expat population: while old-timers tend to frequent the more relaxed ground floor and shuffle along to live classics from the in-house band, newer arrivals are more likely to head downstairs for the trendy white decor, DJ, dancefloor and, obviously, the beach. (While the hungry march straight to the restaurant for some superb bar

Dubai Marina Yacht Club

Barasti

Buddha Bar

food). All, however, can get away with choosing to dress up or don flip flops – Barasti has room for all and that's why it's by far the busiest spot in town. It gets fairly raucous later in the evenings, so if it gets a bit too much, you can choose to head to relative newcomer **Jetty Lounge** back at the One&Only Royal Mirage (see p144). The moment you step in through its own private entrance, you'll know you've come home. There are twinkling Palm Jumeirah lights in the distance, a luminiscent bar and relaxed seating at this cool, classy bar – and yes, it's right by the beach, so you can sit on a lounge chair, sip martinis and crunch the sand beneath your toes.

Tear yourself away from the bar for dinner at **Frankie's** (see p141) back in Dubai Marina. As is often the case with celebrity-driven restaurants, there's a lingering fear of yet another anti-climax waiting to unfold. Happily, Frankie's – the byproduct of a collaboration between Marco Pierre White and jockey Frankie Dettori – is different. It delivers on every front. The atmosphere is lively and vibrant, the food fitting of the restaurant's rich, decadent decor, and the service

is both confident and charming. Try the spaghetti lobster – it's both rich and creamy, without being too heavy. The entire experience will no doubt leave you feeling wholly satisfied… and more than a little spoilt. Stick around for the popular live pianist if you need time to help your food digest and people watch the local expats.

Afterwards, swagger your way into a cab and tell the good man to take you to **Buddha Bar** (see p147) at the Grosvenor House Dubai, also in the Marina. Like it's sister branches throughout the world, its interior screams sophistication with low-level lighting, oriental-themed decor, a gargantuan Buddha dominating the central space and DJs spinning the latest offerings of funky house. The bar staff knock up some killer cocktails and there's plenty of Asian fusion delights on the menu if you're feeling peckish post midnight. A word of warning, though: booking ahead is a must as this place is packed every night of the week, which just goes to show how good it really is. Dance to the oriental and fusion music until the early hours of the morning and raise a toast to Dubai's good life.

Discover the city from your back pocket

Essential for your weekend break, over 30 top cities available.

POCKET SIZED
from £6.99 / $11.95

Dubai by Area

Deira Creek

Deira, Garhoud & Festival City

Deira, Garhoud and Festival City make up a large part of the city which sits on the far side of the mouth of the Creek, where Dubai originally sprung up. Known locally as part of 'Old Dubai', this area was one of the first to be settled by immigrants from the sub-continent and Asia, which gives it a vibrant, bustling flavour, far more akin to other cities in the Middle East, rather than the sometimes sterile feeling of newer areas. Deira can be navigated on foot and visitors should spend an afternoon exploring the souks and tiny restaurants. Traditional dhows jostle for space and while the hotels here are by no means old, you'll get a better rate in this area of town than newer ones.

While a large percentage of the city has evolved, Deira and Garhoud remain resolutely unchanged. For Creek views without the hustle of street vendors, try Festival City – a recent complex of hotels, shops and restaurants alongside a marina.

Deira

Sights & museums

Al Ahmadiya School & Heritage House
Near Gold House building, Al Khor Street, Al Ras (04 226 0286, www. dubai.ae). **Open** 8am-7.30pm Mon-Thur, Sat -Sun; 3pm-7.30pm Fri. **Admission** free. **Map** p66 B1 ●

Established in 1912, Al Ahmadiya was the first school in Dubai and it was renovated as a museum in 1995. Next door lies the Heritage House, a traditional home with interiors dating back to 1890. When you visit, guides and touchscreens will take you through the tour of these two small – and ever so slightly dull – museums.

Dhow Wharfage
Beside Dubai Creek. **Map** p66 B3 ②
A true reminder of the city's past, the Dhow Wharfage along the Deira side of Dubai Creek is where you'll find rows and rows of dhows. These traditional wooden boats bring in spices, textiles and other goods from UAE's neighbours. Even after the decades of development that Dubai's seen, this area still sees quite a bit of activity and makes for a great photo opportunity. You'll also see luxury boats and the modern RTA ferry services competing for your attention with their sleek metal looks and creature comforts (air-conditioning).

Gold Souk
Near Baladiya Street. **Open** 7am-noon, 5-7pm Mon-Thur, Sat, Sun; 5-7pm Fri. **Map** p66 B1 ③
The gold souk is an open market down a wide alley – there's a massive wooden sign above, making it impossible to miss. The walkways lead you past jewellery store upon jewellery store, each with a more ostentatious display than the next, but if you're looking for unique designs, this is the best place to find it. There are a plenty of peddlers on hand ready to sell you snacks, soft drinks and water while you browse, and a few hidden spots where you can find clothing of questionable quality for sale. Towards the eastern end is the perfume souk, in which you can blend your own Arabic-style scents (although they're not to everyone's taste) or purchase copies of designer brand names.

Spice Souk
Near Hyatt Regency, opposite the Gold Souk. **Map** p66 A1 ④
Narrow alleyways lined with sacks and sacks of every spice imaginable welcome your senses here. Be warned though, the souk is a popular tourist attraction, so the prices of many herbs are often laughably high, but barter a bit and you'll see prices come down – the more you buy, the bigger the discount. There's dried lemons and coriander seeds alongside dried rose buds, and regional favourites such as the tangy 'sumac', highly-prized saffron and even herby zaatar, make for great gifts. There's also some good quality oud to be found here – burning a little bit is enough to leave a magical scent in your room for days.

Eating & drinking

Chelsea Arms
Sheraton Dubai Creek Hotel & Towers, Deira, Dubai (04 228 1111). **Open** noon-4pm, 6pm-2am daily. **Pub**. **Map** p66 B2 ⑤
A traditional English pub offering all major sports events on a large screen. If you're a little homesick, this is quite possibly the closest you're going to get to being back home.

China Sea
Al Maktoum Street (04 296 9816). **Open** 11am-2am. **$**. **Chinese**. **Map** p66 B3 ⑥
This much-loved little secret won't be secret for long, now that it has won a *Time Out* Dubai Restaurant Award for its Chinese food. Kooky furniture and Chinese lanterns make for a fun setting, while the dishes will please with not only their authentic taste, but also the sheer size of them.

Delhi Darbar
Sabkha Road, Deira (04 235 6161). **Open** noon-midnight daily. **$**. **Indian**. **Map** p66 B1 ⑦

Deira, Garhoud & Festival City

1 km
1000 yds
© Copyright Time Out Group 2011

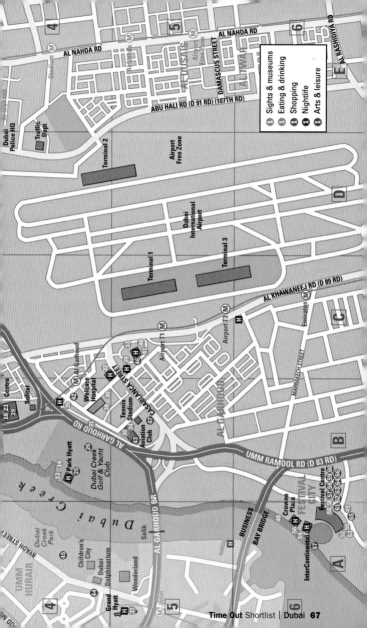

A budget Indian restaurant that has become a bit of a local institution. It's cramped, you're in danger of having your head taken off with the large trays of food the waiters try and balance, but the food is delectable. Waiters are happy to recommend dishes but mention your spice tolerance in advance.

Fish Market

Radisson Blu Hotel, Dubai Deira Creek (04 222 7171). **Open** 12.30pm-3.15pm; 7.30pm-11.15pm daily. **$$$**. **Seafood**. **Map** p66 B3 ⑧

A seafood restaurant with a difference. There's no menu, but choose a fish and decide how you want it cooked and dinner will be served. The tiger prawns are absolutely delicious but watch out for the 'cooking charge'.

Glasshouse Brasserie

Hilton Dubai Creek, Deira (04 212 7551). **Open** 7am-midnight daily. **$$**. **Modern European**. **Map** p66 B3 ⑨

Run by the team behind Gordon Ramsay's Verre restaurant, the Glasshouse has found popularity with its fresh and exciting dishes, for a fraction of the price of Verre. Watch

out for mid-week drinks deals as well, which make it even more appealing.

JW Steakhouse

JW Marriott Dubai, Deira (04 607 7977). **Open** 6pm-midnight daily. **$$$**. **Steakhouse**. **Map** p66 C3 ⑩

JW's is a refined, quiet spot in this grand hotel in Deira. Suitable for serious meat-lovers who want to tackle the enormous cuts, which come with a choice of potato-based sides.

Kisaku

Al Khaleej Palace Hotel, Al Maktoum Road (04 223 1000). **Open** noon-3pm, 6.30pm-midnight daily. **$$**. **Japanese**. **Map** p66 B3 ⑪

A lively, authentic Japanese in the heart of old Dubai. Find plenty of Japanese expats here catching up over generous plates of sashimi, crispy tempura and a mind-boggling array of maki. Wash it down with one of the many sakes on offer.

Shabestan

Radisson Blu Hotel, Baniyas Road, Dubai Deira Creek (04 222 7171). **Open** 12.30-3pm; 7pm-11pm daily. **$$**. **Persian**. **Map** p66 B3 ⑫

Delhi Darbar

Glasshouse Brasserie

Thai Kitchen

One of Dubai's finest Iranian restaurants. Try the Persian kebabs, especially the kebab e soltani – a lamb dish that's succulent and full of flavour, and the nargesi starters.

Thai Kitchen
Park Hyatt Dubai (04 602 1234). **Open** 7pm-midnight daily. **$$$. Thai**. Map p67 B4 ⑬
This beautiful Thai restaurant has been an eternal favourite of many a Time Outer, partly for its stunning Moroccan-inspired terrace, which overlooks a marina chock-a-block with boats, and partly for the delicious and more unusual delights on offer.

Traiteur
Park Hyatt Dubai, Deira (04 317 2222). **Open** 7pm-midnight Sun-Thu; 12.30pm-4pm, 6pm-midnight Fri. **$$$. French**. Map p67 B4 ⑭
Winner of *Time Out Dubai*'s Best Brunch category, this stunning French restaurant is an extremely romantic spot for a quiet meal for two. If you head there to sample the city's brunch obsession, make sure you save

room for their divine hog roast and book a table on the terrace in winter.

Verre by Gordon Ramsay
Hilton Dubai Creek (04 227 1111). **Open** *7pm-midnight Sun-Fri.* **$$$$**. **Fine dining**. Map p66 B3 ⑮
Under Chef Scott Price, who worked with Ramsay in London, Verre is seeing something of a resurgence. Despite the city's fine-dining venues moving towards the marina, Verre has hung on in Old Dubai and is something of a jewel in the crown for the area. At Dhs640 per head, the nine-course chef's table menu is the ticket.

Shopping

Abraj Centre
Sabkha Road (04 221 1479). **Open** 10am-1.30pm, 4.30pm-10.30pm Sat-Thur; 4.30pm-10.30pm Fri. Map p66 B1 ⑯
While we don't condone fur, the number of fur shops cluttered throughout Deira is a truly strange phenomenon – especially when it's 50 degrees outside and the sight of fur

DUBAI BY AREA

Fish Market

Deira City Centre

brings on nausea, even in those not concerned with the fates of critters. Abraaj Centre is a particular hot spot.

Brands for Less
Al Bakhit Centre (04 266 9657). **Open** 10am-11pm daily. **Map** p66 C3 ⑰
This bargain basement-style store stocks many brands on the cheap – we've picked up a fair few finds – from Levi's to Steve Madden.

Deira City Centre
Port Saeed Road (04 295 4545). **Open** 10am-10pm Sun-Wed; 10am-midnight Thur-Sat. **Map** p66 B4 ⑱
This large mall is one of the oldest in Dubai and is always crowded. It's a real high-street haven, but is also home to Iconic (see below), as well as some other high-end brands.

Fish market
Opposite Hyatt Regency Dubai & Galleria. **Open** 9am-1pm, 4pm-10pm Sat-Thur; 4pm-10pm Fri. **Map** p66 B1 ⑲
A huge hall contains stall upon stall of fresh fish, as an army of men in blue uniforms rush around boxing, weighing and carving up the day's catch. While splashing your path past the stalls – this is not a place for flip-flops – expect to see black hammour, koffer, kingfish, safi, shark and plenty of brawny king prawns.

Fruit & vegetable souk
Opposite Hyatt Regency Dubai & Galleria. **Open** 9am-1pm, 4pm-10pm Sat-Thur; 4pm-10pm Fri. **Map** p66 B1 ⑳
If you enter here from the adjoining meat market, it's like dying and being reborn. Bright, colourful and fragrant, with an upbeat aura, it's a fun place to look around even if you have no intention on stocking up on fresh goods. Pick up some ice-cold coconut water to keep you refreshed.

Gift Village
Baniyas Square (04 294 6858). **Open** 9am-1am Sat-Thur; 9am-12pm, 2pm-2am Fri. **Map** p66 B2 ㉑
This mall in Deira is a bargain hunter's dream – electronics are particularly cheap and it's full of one man's tat – suitcases, toys, clothes, souvenirs – another man's treasure.

Gold Souk

frankincense. With many malls and supermarkets now offering spices, the livelihood of the characters here is under threat, so get shopping!

Arts & leisure

Amara Spa

Park Hyatt Dubai (04 602 1660, www.dubai.park.hyatt.com). **Open** 9am-10pm daily. **Map** p67 B4 25

Moroccan-themed decor, private outdoor rain showers, a palm tree-lined pool, a steam room and a fantastic food menu, there's enough to do for the whole day here, even if you're kicking back and relaxing.

Gold Souk

Sikkat al-Khail Street, Deira. **Open** 10am-10pm Sat-Thur; 4pm-10pm Fri. **Map** p66 B1 22

Even if you don't plan on buying anything, a stroll through this yellow-gold lined market street is a must-do. Explore the side alleys as well, where you'll find more unusual stores as well as clusters of fresh fruit stalls.

Iconic

Port Saeed Road (04 294 3444). **Open** 10am-10pm Sun-Wed; 10am-midnight Thur-Sat. **Map** p67 B4 23

Spread over two floors, this is Deira City Centre's (one of Dubai's older malls) flagship store. There are over 130 brands in store, ranging from womenswear and menswear to electronics and trinkets – there's even a salon to groom mid-peruse.

Spice Souk

Near the Hyatt Regency, opposite the Gold Souk. **Open** daily from sunrise. **Map** p66 B1 24

Wander through these cramped alleyways to pick up a range of spices – from saffron to dried lemons and

Dubai Creek Golf & Yacht Club

Next to Park Hyatt (04 295 6000, www.dubaigolf.com). **Open** 7am-2.00pm daily. **Map** p67 B4 26

One of the oldest courses in Dubai, it's in a central location in the middle of the city and makes a welcome change from some of the desert courses. A first-class green (the nine-hole par three course is floodlit), it offers facilities to match its dhow-inspired clubhouse. Twilight golf rates are Dhs420 (weekdays) and Dhs480 (weekends), from 3pm onwards.

Emirates Billiards Centre

Near Ramada Continental Hotel (04 262 4499). **Open** 10am-4am Sat-Thur; 2pm-4am Fri. **Map** p66 E3 27

Get a late night pool session in at this local haunt, it has 11 tables, so book ahead to secure a game. Dhs15 an hour before 7pm, Dhs30 thereafter.

Dubai International Bowling Centre

Next to Century Mall (04 296 9222). **Open** 9am-1am daily. **Map** p66 E3 28

Dubai's Bowling HQ has a grand total of 36 lanes plus pool tables. It costs Dhs100 per lane, per hour Thur-Fri; Sat 9am-noon Dhs12 per person; noon-1am Dhs15 per person.

DUBAI BY AREA

Vox Cinemas

Deira City Centre (04 294 9000). **Open** 10am-10pm daily. **Map** p67 B4 ㉙

Showing the latest films and movies plus gold class screenings, where you sit on a La-Z-Boy chair and press a button to order popcorn and cooked foods such as burgers and fries. Other branches include Mall of the Emirates

Garhoud

Eating & drinking

Abajour

523rd Street (04 283 4556). **Open** 8am-1am daily. **$. Middle Eastern.** **Map** p67 B4 ㉚

The Syrian eatery has a devoted following who go every night to smoke, eat, socialise and listen to the live Arabic music. Service is prompt, friendly and the menu offers the standard dishes, as well as a few more adventurous options, such as sparrow, and some creative shakes.

Al Hallab

Near to Chili's (04 341 1880). **Open** noon-11pm daily. **$. Lebanese.** **Map** p67 B4 ㉛

Dubai's not short of Lebanese restaurants but Al Hallab is a stalwart. Eat in, or order some delivery if you're in the area, their cheese mannakines are legendary and huge. Inexpensive, tasty and filling – what more do you need?

Biggles

Millennium Airport Hotel (04 282 3464). **Open** noon-2am Sat-Thur; 11am-2am Fri. **$. Pub. Map** p67 C4 ㉜

Bypassing the bizarre decor (there appears to be a mummified parachutist dangling from the ceiling), Biggles is the epitome of English pub. It's arguably a match-day haunt, with three plasma screens that have just about every angle covered – the centrepiece screen is positively

massive – and there's a fair few regulars to be found at the bar.

Café Chic

Le Méridien (04 217 0000). **Open** 12.30pm-3.30pm, 7pm-midnight daily. **$$$. French. Map** p67 C5 ㉝

Quiet and refined French restaurant that still hasn't quite hit the radar of most foodies yet. Think veal, lobster, various carpaccios and the restaurant has half a dozen signature souffles, we love the strawberry one.

The Cellar

The Aviation Club (04 282 4122). **Open** noon-1am daily. **$$. Modern European/Bar.** **Map** p67 B5 ㉞

More sleek restaurant than damp basement, Gothic-style eatery The Cellar provides an upmarket option in Garhoud, with separate dining room and bar menus. Mains in the restaurant are more edgy and interesting, try the beef fillet with garlic snails!

India Palace

Opposite Fuddruckers (04 286 9600). **Open** noon-midnight daily. **$. Indian.** **Map** p67 B4 ㉟

The dark wood and slightly dusty atmosphere somehow suits this old-style Indian restaurant. The outside might not look like much, but the food is superb. Chicken tikka comes expertly charred while naans are thin and crispy.

The Irish Village

The Aviation Club (04 282 4750). **Open** 11am-1am Fri-Tue; 11am-2.45am Wed-Thur. **$. Pub. Map** p67 B5 ㊱

An absolute Dubai institution, this huge al fresco mock Irish pub offers hearty grub, such as bangers and mash, on long wooden tables. In winter, expats flock here to make the most of the outside space, while the venue puts on gigs, comedy nights and mini beer festivals throughout the year. Always worth a visit.

More

iZ

Grand Hyatt Dubai (04 317 2400).
Open 12.30pm-3.30pm daily, 7pm-
12.30pm Sat-Wed; 7pm-1am Thur-Fri.
$$$. **Indian**. Map p67 A5 ③⑦
One of the finest (and most expensive)
Indian restaurants in the city, the
live cooking stations will whip up a
storm, with a daily changing menu.
The prawn masala should be tried if
you're here, but if you want a cheaper
option, come for lunch and try the
tapas-style menu.

More

*Behind Welcare Hospital (04 283
0224).* **Open** 7am-7pm daily. **$$**. **Café**.
Map p67 B4 ③⑨
This chain of cafés now stretches
right across Dubai, but this is where
it all started. With a vast menu of
home-cooked dishes, ranging from
South African hotpots to curries,
pastries and burgers. Free Wi-Fi and
complimentary magazines makes
More a useful spot for a solo traveller.

Rodeo Grill

Al Bustan Rotana (04 282 0000). **Open**
noon-3pm; 7pm-midnight daily. **$$$**.
Steakhouse. Map p67 C5 ③⑨

Rodeo Grill goes above and beyond
the normal steakhouse, in addition
to a wide range of cuts and wagyu,
it offers creative sauce options
and interesting combinations which
raise its game.

Warehouse

Le Méridien (04 282 4040). **Open** 5pm-
1.30am Sat-Thur; 1pm-4pm, 5pm-1.30am
Fri. **$$**. **Asian/Bar**. Map p67 C5 ④⓪
This diverse bar, restaurant and club
offers a range of options. From the
wine bar and outside terrace for post-
work drinks, move on to the fusion
Asian restaurant upstairs, then round
off the night by hitting the dancefloor
and whiskey bar.

Yalumba

Le Méridien (04 217 0000). **Open** 7pm-
10pm Wed-Mon, 8pm-11pm Tues. **$$**.
Australian. Map p67 C5 ④①
Sunday to Thursday, Yalumba is a
respectable Australian restaurant,
serving up plenty of salads, steaks
and seafood. But come Friday, it's the
location of the most raucous brunch in
town – a legend in its own right. Not a
place for a quiet weekend but if you're
looking for a party, head here.

DUBAI BY AREA

Shopping

Party Centre

Opposite Welcare Hospital (04 283 1353). **Open** 9am-9pm Sat-Thur; 3pm-9pm Fri. **Map** p67 B4 ㊷

This massive store is perfect if you're throwing a birthday party while you're in Dubai. It has hundreds of quirky balloon designs, costumes and, well, literally anything you could ever need when planning a shindig.

Arts & leisure

Akaru Spa

Aviation Club, Garhoud (04 282 8578, www.akaruspa.com). **Open** 10am-10pm daily. **Map** p67 B5 ㊸

A reliable spa specialising in facials, body wraps and a holistic approach to health. The spa also offers various weight-loss treatments and has a gym and an outdoor pool attached.

Dubai Dolphinarium

Creek Park, Gate 1, Umm Hurair 2, nr Garhoud Bridge, (04 336 9773, www.dubaidolphinarium.ae). **Open** 10am-8pm Mon-Sat. **Map** p67 A4 ㊹

Live dolphin, seal and acrobatic shows take place every day and evening inside Creek Park. Dolphins flick balls with their tails, splash the audience and play with hoops and balls as part of an atmospheric performance. The whole experience is quite old fashioned, it's up to you whether you're ok with that or whether you prefer your dolphins to be seen frolicking in the wild.

Creek Park

Al Riyadh Street, between Garhoud Bridge and Floating Bridge (04 336 7633). **Open** 2pm-11.30pm Sun-Wed; 8am-11pm Thur-Sat. **Map** p67 A4 ㊺

You'll never get bored during a visit to this sprawling waterside space. Activities on offer include several children's playgrounds, bike rental (Dhs30 an hour), a park train to guide you around the area and an 18-hole mini golf course. There's also the huge Children's City, which is full of educational activities and displays for kids (entry is Dhs10 for kids, Dhs15 for adults). You can also bring your fishing rod (it's actually encouraged), and they'll let you cast off from the jetty by the creek. It's also home to the older style Dolphinarium.

Natural Elements Spa & Fitness

Le Méridien Dubai, Garhoud (04 702 2550, www.dubai.lemeridien.com). **Open** 6am-10pm daily. **Map** p67 C5 ㊻

The warm reception, scented rooms and accomplished therapists make this a winning spot for a massage. Facials start at Dhs360.

SNTTA Tours

Garhoud (04 286 5758). **Open** 8.30am-6pm Sat-Thur. **Map** p67 B5 ㊼

Had enough of the city lights? This tour agency offers dinner experiences, dune bashing, sand-skiing, camel rides, as well as an overnight safari and a tour of the UAE's east coast. Call for prices.

Festival City

Eating & drinking

Belgian Beer Café

Crowne Plaza Festival City (04 701 2222). **Open** 6pm-1am Sat-Thur; Fri 1pm-4pm, 6pm-1am. **$$**. **Bar**. **Map** p67 A6 ㊽

Belgian Beer Café (or BBC) is as close to an upmarket gastro-pub as you're going to get. The double doors hide a dark wooden interior, complete with Belgian knick-knacks hanging from the ceiling and a smoky atmosphere which makes it feel rather authentic. Order a speciality beer and grab a table on the terrace in the winter months to watch the sun set over Dubai's iconic skyline.

One man's trash...

Second-hand shopping has never been easier.

Over the last couple of years, Dubai's market culture has been given a breath of life, having taken a hit when the city began building mall after air-conditioned mall. The newer kids on the block are, however, garnering an increasingly large following. For sure, the market scene isn't what it was and on the surface there are few bargains to be had, but if you look a little closer, brush up your bargaining skills and be clear on what you're looking for, it's possible to find exactly what you want for the right price. From October until May, the city's newest market, Covent Garden Market (as you may have noticed with places such as The Dubai Mall and the Dubai Fountains, the city isn't first for creative naming) is open 5pm to midnight, every evening, from Wednesday to Saturday.

Positioned along The Walk, the beachfront promenade of Jumeirah Beach Residence, a place stuffed liberally with cafés and restaurants (unlicensed, except in the few hotels), the market has proved a pulling point for both locals and tourists, and is a great place to pick up Arabic script and evil eye jewellery for a good price.

Busier yet is the monthly Dubai Flea Market, the city's only answer to a car boot sale, which you'll find stationed in Safa Park during cooler months and at various indoor venues in the summer (check website for upcoming details). Venture to this perennially popular second-hand market to discover a world where people have no concept of queuing, where a complete stranger will haggle with you over Dhs1 and where some vendors will try to sell half-empty VCR box sets of '90s TV shows featuring the ginger dude from *CSI*. But, it's also a place where you'll find original artwork for less than Dhs200, the latest *Grey's Anatomy* series for Dhs10 and retro costume jewellery that would rival your nan's much loved collection.

Also worth a look is the ARTE Souk in Times Square Centre, just off Dubai's arterial Sheikh Zayed Road. Selling everything from cushion covers and handbag organisers to jewellery, there are plenty of interesting and unique pieces to be found.

Year-round markets in Dubai, such as Deira's gold souk, spice souk and the fruit, vegetable and fish market offer good value all the time. You'll find fresh, low-cost produce and the opportunity to buy jewellery tax-free. Check out www.dubai-fleamarket.com, www.coventgardenmarket.ae and www.arte.ae.

DUBAI BY AREA

Belgian Beer Café p74

Jamie's Italian

Blades

Al Badia Golf Course (04 701 1128).
Open 5.30pm-1am daily. **$$$**.
International. Map p67 A6 ❹
This signature restaurant is known
for its interesting American dishes,
such as a New York strip loin with
mango and sweet chilli sauce. One
of the few restaurants in Dubai that
overlooks a green space, even if you're
not in the mood for golf, it's worth
swinging by.

Chi'Zen

Marina Promenade (04 232 9077).
Open noon-midnight daily. **$$$**.
Chinese. Map p67 A6 ❺
Chi'Zen burst onto the culinary scene
earlier this year with a flourish and it
offers high end, modern Chinese fare
with really exceptional ingredients.
Definitely no MSG or gloopy orange
sauces in sight.

Jamie's Italian

Festival Centre (04 232 9969). **Open**
noon-1am Thur-Sat; noon-midnight Sun.
$$. **Italian**. Map p67 A6 ❺
The much-loved British chef's first
restaurant in the Middle East, it's a

funky, industrial-styled venue with
surprisingly reasonably priced food.
Try the bruschetta with pumpkin for
starters and the salmon steak for a
main course.

Le Relais d' Entrecôte

*Al Rebat Street, Festival City (04 232
5208).* **Open** 12.30pm-11.30pm daily.
$$. **French**. Map p67 A6 ❺
A quaint little French restaurant
with amazing views from the terrace
at any time other than summer. It
offers a selection of salad starters,
followed by the namesake l'entrecote
and frites.

Mamma Oliva

Festival Centre (04 232 8622). **Open**
noon-10pm Sat-Wed; noon-midnight.
Thu-Fri. **$$**. **Italian**.
Map p67 A6 ❺
The location has quirk value – you
can sit on an outdoor table on a
bridge over the Festival Centre canal
within the Festival City mall. The
pizza base is fresh and tasty, but little
else justifies the sometimes rather
large bill. You can order a raw pizza
where toppings come cold, a virgin

Reflets par Pierre Gagnaire

olive oil pizza or stick with more traditional, crispy base options.

Reflets par Pierre Gagnaire

InterContinental Festival City (04 701 1111). **Open** noon-3.30pm, 7pm-11.30pm Mon-Fri. **$$$$**. **Fine dining**. **Map** p67 A6 54

Time Out Dubai's 2011 Restaurant of the Year, this worthy winner is in a league of its own, with the experimental culinary skills of Pierre Gagnaire inspiring the journey-style menus that change regularly. This is an absoultely five star evening, and remember to indulge in the skills of the sommelier.

Spur

Festival Centre (04 232 8866). **Open** 10am-10.30pm Sat-Wed; 10am-midnight Thur-Fri. **$$**. **Steakhouse**. **Map** p67 A6 55

This reasonably priced steakhouse has found favour with families out shopping at the weekend. No fuss and not too many frills, the South African chain brings a touch more class to the usual mall restaurants.

Vista Lounge & Bar

InterContinental Festival City (04 701 1111).**Open** 6pm-2am daily. **$$**. **Bar**. **Map** p67 A6 56

A stunning lounge and piano bar that offers views right across the Dubai Creek as well as the marina. Definitely worth a sundowner or two, if you're in the area.

Shopping

Ace Hardware

Dubai Festival City (800 275 223). **Open** 9am-10pm Sat-Wed; 9am-midnight Thur-Fri. **Map** p67 A6 57

Dubai's best hardware store is a mammoth building, where you'll find everything you need to renovate as well as quirkier finds, such as a large range of tropical fish.

The Fashion Net

First floor, Dubai Festival Centre (04 232 9540). **Open** 10am-10pm Sun-Wed; 10am-midnight Thur-Sat. **Map** p67 A6 58

This new multi-brand independent boutique focuses on fashion from Italy and Spain – expect lots of

DUBAI BY AREA

colour, girly party dresses and easy breezy, casual beachwear.

Ferrari Store

Dubai Festival Centre (04 232 9845). **Open** 10am-10pm Sun-Wed; 10am-midnight Thur-Sat. **Map** p67 A6 ⊕

The largest store in the world to sell everything to do with the prancing horse (besides the cars), the 1,000-square-metres of space stocks all sorts of memorabilia and also has some interactive elements. A must for any Ferrari fan (as is the fairly new Ferrari World in Abu Dhabi).

Gold Marketplace

Dubai Festival Centre (04 232 5444). **Open** 10am-10pm Sun-Wed; 10am-midnight Thur-Sat. **Map** p67 A6 ⊕

This in-mall jewellery marketplace features dozens of shops keen to sell everything from titanium rings to diamond earrings. While not as plentiful as the other gold souks around town, it's so quiet that you'll often cut a good deal.

Magrudy's

Dubai Festival Centre (04 232 8761). **Open** 10am-10pm Sun-Wed; 10am-midnight Thur-Sat. **Map** p67 A6 ⊕

This chain of bookstores began trading in 1975, when it opened its first (still open) Jumeirah store and it has since become a favourite spot for Dubai expats. This, one of the newer branches, is fantastic because it's mammoth and there are a lot of local interest books that are worth checking out if you want to learn more about the region.

Mumbai Se

Dubai Festival Centre (04 232 6070). **Open** 10am-10pm Sun-Wed; 10am-midnight Thur-Sat. **Map** p67 A6 ⊕

This Indian fashion boutique stocks a range of contemporary and traditional clothes for women in the brightest selection of silks you'll find this side of Rajahstan. While not to everyone's taste, the local and Indian clothes are worth a look – if you find something, it's sure to be a one-off back home.

SkinJam

Stall nr indoor waterfall, Dubai Festival Centre (04 232 5444). **Open** 10am-10pm Sun-Wed; 10am-midnight Thur-Sat. **Map** p67 A6 ⊕

The UAE likes to customise everything – from license plates to cars and mobile phones. SkinJam is the place to give your phone, laptop and more a makeover. If you're really brave, go for a fully crystalised option.

Magrudy's

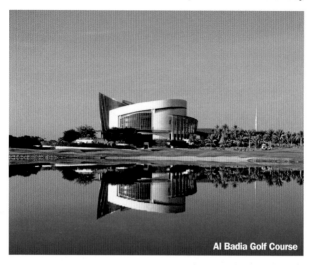

Al Badia Golf Course

DUBAI BY AREA

Trade Routes

Dubai Festival Centre (04 232 5444).
Open 10am-10pm Sun-Wed; 10am-
midnight Thur-Sat. **Map** p67 A6 ➏➍
This 'marketplace' sits on the mini
creek outside Dubai Festival Centre
and sells carpets and other such
Arabian (and Persian) treasures.
The shops are quiet, so prices are
sometimes lowered to a good rate
(however touristy spots are always
going to be more expensive than back
alley warehouse shops in Sharjah
and Deira).

Arts & leisure

Al Badia Golf Course

*Al Rebat Street (04 601 0101, www.
albadiagolfclub.ae).* **Open** 6.30am-5pm
(last tee for nine holes); 2.50pm (last tee
for 18 holes) daily. **Map** p67 A6 ➏➎
Challenging 18-hole course with
floodlit driving range and extras,
including MATT swing analysis
and a Science and Motion putting
laboratory (SAM PuttLab). Also
features a steakhouse, Terra Firma.

Bowling City

*Festival Centre, Dubai Festival City
(04 232 8600, www.bowling-city.com).*
Open 10am-midnight Sat-Thur; 10am-
1am Fri. **Map** p67 A6 ➏➏
With centres across the UAE, Bowling
City's flagship branch, located slap-
bang in the middle of Festival Centre,
has brought the brand into the heart
of Dubai. Featuring 12 lanes and
nine pool tables (not forgetting four
karaoke cabins), Bowling City is a
haven for close-skilled sports, offering
multiple distractions in one venue.

Intercontinental Festival City Spa

*Intercontinental Festival City (04
701 1111, www.ichotelsgroup.com/
intercontinental/en/gb/spa/dubai-
festivalcity).* **Open** 8am-10pm daily.
Map p67 A6 ➏➐
VIP treatment rooms, spa ritual
afternoons, heavenly facials, couples'
massages and more, means this is one
spot you can guarantee that will melt
away any travelling tension. There's
often discounted treatments too.

Gold Souq

Bur Dubai & Oud Metha

Across the creek from Deira and Garhoud sits the other half of 'Old Dubai': Bur Dubai and Oud Metha. Bur Dubai's charm is its relatively old-style architecture, mostly built in the '70s and the '80s. It remains a place for a cheap night out, as long as you don't mind the odd seedy bar and a hit-and-miss approach to covers bands. Once the place where the ruling families made their home along the southern banks of the creek, visitors can now find the Dubai Museum, which gives an insight into how Dubai came to life through traditional pearl diving and trading. Bur Dubai's port is still extremely active to this day, within its shadow now sits Bastakiya, a reformed heritage area which has

recreated traditional buildings that house art galleries and independent cafés. Only accessible on foot, this area gives some perspective on how far Dubai has come in only a few decades.

Bur Dubai

Sights & museums

Creek crossing
End of Al Seef Road, nr entrance of Bastakiya souk, Dubai Creek (800 9090, www.rta.ae). **Open** 5am-midnight. **Map** p82 D4 ❶
The cheapest way to view the Creek is on one of the abras (traditional wooden boats). These rickety, but

watertight boats have been ferrying people across the creek since Dubai began. Originally, they were row boats, but now they're motorised, and thousands of people cross the creek on them every day. With fares starting at just Dhs1, peak times, as you can imagine, are chaotic and it's worth hiring a whole abra for a more personal experience. Make sure you agree on the cost and length of the tour with the captain before setting out – a journey up and down the Creek should cost no more than Dhs50. You also have the option of taking a more modern water taxi – in the comfort of reclining seats and air-conditioning, these taxis can ferry you all the way to Palm Jumeirah and Dubai Marina.

Bastakiya

*Between Al Fahidi Street and
the southern bank of Dubai Creek.*
Map p82 D2 ②
One of Dubai's most picturesque heritage sights, Bastakiya has been carefully renovated over the years. The name Bastakiya comes from the first people to settle the area, traders from Bastak in southern Iran. The ruler of Dubai encouraged immigration in the early 1900s by granting favourable tax concessions, and many people came and stayed, which explains why so many Emiratis are of southern Iranian descent. Walking through the narrow alleyways can feel like a step into Dubai's past, even though few of the buildings and wind towers are original. Here, you'll find the Sheikh Mohammed Centre for Cultural Understanding, a few art galleries, as well as a boutique hotel and a charming courtyard café. Well worth a leisurely stroll.

Dubai Museum

*Al Fahidi Fort, Bastakiya (04 353 1862,
www.dubai.ae).* **Open** 8.30am-8.30pm
Mon-Thur, Sat, Sun; 2.30-8.30pm Fri.
Admission Dhs3. **Map** p82 D2 ❸
If you know little about Arab history, Dubai's museum is definitely worth a visit. The Al Fahidi Fort was built in 1787 as Dubai's primary sea defence and also served as the ruler's residence. In 1970 it was renovated so

Dubai Creek

DUBAI BY AREA

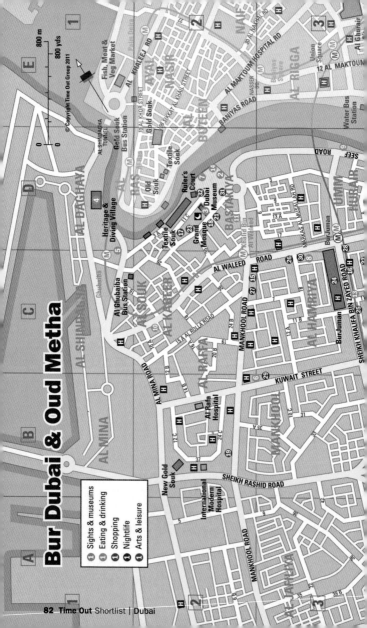

Bur Dubai & Oud Metha

- ⓵ Sights & museums
- ⓵ Eating & drinking
- ⓵ Shopping
- ⓵ Nightlife
- ⓵ Arts & leisure

Fish, Meat & Veg Market

Heritage & Diving Village

Gold Souk Bus Station

Gold Souk

AL SHINDAGHA TUNNEL

Textile Souk

Old Souk

Ruler's Court

Grand Mosque

Dubai Museum

Al Ghubaiba Bus Station

AL WALEED ROAD

MANKHOOL ROAD

AL ROLLA ROAD

BurJuman

KUWAIT STREET

At-Rafa Hospital

New Gold Souk

International Modern Hospital

SHEIKH RASHID ROAD

AL WHALEEJ RD

AL KHOR STREET

BANIYAS ROAD

AL MAKTOUM HOSPITAL RD

AL MAKTOUM RD

AL NAKHEEL RD

AL MUSALLA RD

UNION SQUARE

12 AL MAKTOUM

AL RIGGA

Water Bus Station

SEEF ROAD

SHEIKH KHALIFA BIN ZAYED ROAD

800 m
800 yds

© Copyright Time Out Group 2011

RIGGAT
AL BUTEEN

AL RIGGA

Al Garhoud

AL GARHOUD RD

Welcare
Hospital

Deira City
Centre

Sofitel

City Centre

ROCCOSNAR
ROUNDABOUT

Park Hyatt

Dubai Creek
Golf & Yacht
Club

Dhow
Wharfage

Salik

MAKTOUM BR

FLOATING BR

Dubai Creek

Water Bus
Station

Dubai
Courts

RYADH STREET

Dubai
Creek
Park

TARIQ BIN ZIYAD

Rashid
Hospital

Children's
City

Dubai
Dolphinarium

UMM HURAIR

ZA'ABEEL ROAD

UMM HURAIR

Oud Metha

OUD METHA

Lulu Centre

Emirates
Post

Karama
Park

Health City

DUBAI
HEALTH CARE
CITY

AL KARAMA

40 Al Wasl
Leisureland

56
35 53

American
Hospital

Raffles

Wafi City

34 39 43 46 47

OUD METHA

37 42 55 60

49 50 51 52

Hospital

Karama
Shopping
Complex

20

41

Lamcy
Plaza

45

38

36

Mövenpick

44 57

Al Wasl
Hospital

55A

SHEIKH RASHID ROAD

Za'abeel
Park

OUD METHA RD (E66)

33 59

Al Jafiliya

ZA'ABEEL 1

AL KIFAF

TRADE CENTRE
ROUNDABOUT

Bastakiya

Basta Art Café

the museum could be housed within its walls. Inside, the displays are creative and imaginative, allowing you to peek into Bedouin life, right through to the pearl diving days with detailed exhibits and videos. Nearby, you'll also find the Grand Mosque. It was constructed over a decade ago to resemble the original Grand Mosque that was built around 1900 in the same location and doubled as a religious school. Sadly, the first Grand Mosque was torn down in the '60s.

Heritage & Diving Village

Al Shindagha (04 393 7151, www. dubai.ae). **Open** 8.30am-10pm Sat-Thur; 8am-11am, 4pm-10pm Fri. **Admission** free. **Map** p82 D1 ❹

Best described as a 'living' museum, you'll find potters, weavers and other craftspeople here. It focuses on Dubai's maritime past and depicts the life and times of seafarers who farmed the waters of the Gulf for pearls and fish. There's a tented village that provides an insight into the Bedouin way of life, which remained unchanged until well into the 20th

Century. Call ahead to find out if there are any traditional ceremonies and shows on – sword dancing and wedding celebrations occur regularly on public holidays and during special events, such as the Dubai Shopping Festival.

Sheikh Saeed Al Maktoum House

Al Shindagha (04 393 7139, www. dubai.ae). **Open** 8am-8:30pm Sat-Thur; 3:30pm-9:30pm Fri. **Admission** Dhs1. **Map** p82 D1 ❺

Built in 1896 out of coral, then covered in lime and sand plaster, this traditional house was the home of Dubai's ruler until his death in 1958. It's a beautiful example of regional architecture, with wind towers and rooms built around a central courtyard. The house has a strategic position at the mouth of the creek, where the ruler could observe shipping activity from the balconies. It's now a museum that hosts small exhibits of old documents, stamps, currencies and a collection of old photographs of Dubai and its ruling family.

Eating & drinking

Aangan
Dhow Palace Hotel (04 359 9992).
Open noon-3.30pm, 7pm-2am daily. **$$**.
Indian. Map p82 B2 ⑥
Time Out Dubai's winner for Best Indian, this unassuming restaurant serves up consistently great food, without breaking the bank. A great place to kick-start a night of music bars in Bur Dubai.

Basta Art Café
Fahidi Street (04 353 5071).
Open 8am-10pm daily. **$**. **Café**. Map p82 D2 ⑦
Set in among the art galleries of the Bastakiya area, this shady courtyard offers a range of delicious salads, Arabic sandwiches and tasty juices. Popular, especially in the winter months, this place is usually a buzzing place to visit.

Bastakiah Nights
3C Street (04 353 7772). **Open** 11am-10.30pm daily. **$**. **Arabic**. Map p82 C3 ⑧
An experience in its own right, set on a beautiful terrace in the heart of Bur Dubai, this Arabic restaurant promises much. Meals can be hit-and-miss, but for fresh juices and shisha, it can't be beaten.

Bateaux Dubai
Opposite British Embassy, Al Seef Road (04 399 4994). **Open** 8.30pm-11pm daily. **$$$**. **Modern European**.
Map p82 D3 ⑨
This Creek cruise has really pulled the stops out recently to offer a stylish modern European menu that would impress on and off the water. Glide through Old Dubai at night while you're entertained with traditional music and dancing.

Casa de Goa
Palm Beach Hotel, Khalid Bin Al Waleed Road (04 393 1999). **Open** noon-3.30pm, 7pm-1am daily. **$$**. **Indian**.
Map p82 C2 ⑩
Tucked away in the incongruously named Palm Beach Hotel, this authentic little hideaway offers a solid menu of traditional Goan dishes, where the seafood shines through. Inexpensive, it's a real diamond in the Bur Dubai rough.

Goodfellas
Regal Plaza (04 355 6633). **Open** noon-3am daily. **$**. **Italian**. Map p82 D2 ⑪
For a slice of underground action in Dubai, head over to this busy sports bar and prepare to jostle for elbow space at the bar. It's by no means a place to spend a romantic evening, but it's always good for a crowd.

Bateaux Dubai

DUBAI BY AREA

Sukh Sagar

Bur Dubai Souk

Paratha King

Hilal building, opposite the GPO (04 396 2114). **Open** 8am-3pm, 7pm-11pm Sat-Thur; 7pm-11pm Fri. **$**. No credit cards. **Indian**. Map p83 C4

This Indian fast food bolt-hole in Karama is a popular spot to fill up for only a few dirhams. Over 100 options of the filled flat bread are on offer, all vegetarian, and each come with dahl or curd. You might need the latter to calm down any spicy choices.

Sukh Sagar

Sheikh Khalifa bin Zayed Road (04 396 7222). **Open** 9am-midnight daily. **$**. **Indian**. Map p82 C3 ⑬

One of Dubai's longest running restaurants (it's been open since 1962), this vegetarian Indian budget place has expanded to offer some Italian and Chinese dishes, but it's best to stick to the original fare. Nothing fancy, but for cheap Indian food you can't go wrong.

XVA Café

Bastakiya (04 353 5383). **Open** 9am-7pm Sat-Thur; 10am-5pm Fri. **$**. **Café**. Map p82 D2 ⑭

This little boutique café also doubles up as a hotel and art gallery. It's one of the few vegetarian places in the city, so settle down into the cute, cool courtyard and get stuck into a smoothie and some people-watching.

Shopping

Al Ain Centre

Mankhool Road, Mankhool, Bur Dubai (04 352 5075). **Open** 10am-10pm daily. Map p82 C2 ⑮

Home to 'Computer Plaza', where you'll find all manner of geeky gadgetry, but few know that inside the actual centre you'll find several silver jewellery kiosks – prices here are a bargain and some of the designs are unique.

Avenue

Ground Floor, Al Kifaf Building, Trade Centre Road opposite BurJuman (04 397 9983). **Open** 9.30am-11pm Thur-Sat; 4.30pm-11pm Fri. Map p82 C3 ⑯

A mini department store, you can stock up on cosmetics, shoes, accessories, home linen and rather questionable fashion for the entire family here.

Saks Fifth Avenue

Bur Dubai Souk

*Al Fahidi Street next to the abra station
(04 353 1465).* **Open** 10am-10pm Sat-
Thur; 4pm-10pm Fri. **Map** p82 D2 ⑰
A must-do. Experience the buzzing
atmosphere of 'Old Dubai', buy
trinkets, such as slippers and fabric,
and make sure to fill up on samosas,
pakoras, bhaji and the like for just
Dhs10 from Al Shaab Restaurant.

Dreamgirls

Meena Bazaar (04 352 6463). **Open**
4pm-10pm Sat-Thur; 6pm-9pm Fri.
Map p82 D2 ⑱
This tailor's so good, one of the
Time Out Dubai team got their
wedding dress made there (for less
than Dhs1,500). It's a large shop with
many tailors, so find someone you're
comfortable with if you're getting
something made.

Fabindia

*Nashwan Building, Al Mankhool Road
(04 398 9633).* **Open** 10am-10pm Sat-
Thur; 4pm-10pm Fri. **Map** p82 B2 ⑲
A local favourite, this store sells
beautiful textiles from India. Buy
yourself colourful throws and
cushions, as well as some nifty outfits.

If you're heading on through to the
subcontinent, don't bother with it,
however, as it is more expensive.

Karama Shopping Complex

Central Karama. **Open** 10am-10pm Sat-
Thur; 4pm-10pm Fri. **Map** p83 B4 ⑳
This series of shopping squares
is famous for copy watches, fake
handbags and the like. If you want to
look at copies of the exclusive brands,
you'll be whisked off to secret rooms
via fake walls and doors.

Meena Bazaar

*Near Khalid bin Waleed Road, Bur
Dubai.* **Open** 10am-10pm Sat-Thur;
4pm-10pm Fri. **Map** p82 D2 ㉑
This hard to find market is the place to
pick up textiles in the city – the shops,
run mostly by Indian expatriates, are
filled with everything from polyester
to delicious silks.

Ohm Records

*Al Kifaf Building, Sheikh Khalifa bin
Zayed Road, Karama (04 397 3728).*
Open 9am-6pm Sun-Thur. **Map** p82
C3 ㉒
One of Dubai's only vinyl record
stores, this institution also sells

DUBAI BY AREA

DJ equipment, and the company organises a range of muso night events throughout the city.

Perfector Electronics

Al Fahidi Street (04 353 1786). **Open** 9am-1.30pm, 4.30pm-10pm Sat-Thur; 4.30pm-9pm Fri. **Map** p82 D2 ㉓
This electronics shop has a fantastic camera selection that's often cheaper than what's on offer in the big malls.

Saks Fifth Avenue

BurJuman (04 351 5551). **Open** 10am-11pm Sat-Wed; 10am-midnight Thur-Sat. **Map** p82 C3 ㉔
On the first level, you'll find all of life's not-so-necessary niceties – cosmetics and fragrances, designer sunglasses, and the D&G Boutique – but level two is where shopping gets serious. Missoni, Issey Miyake, Prada and John Galliano fill up the racks.

Nightlife

Club Se7en

Park Regis Kris Kin Hotel (04 37 1111, www.staywellgroup.com). **Open** 6pm-3am daily. **Map** p82 C3 ㉕
A new arrival on the live music scene, Club Se7en follows the tried and tested cover band route, but has also played host to alternative nights playing funk, soul and hip hop.

Elegante

Royal Ascot Hotel (04 352 0900). **Open** 10pm-3am daily. **Map** p82 C3 ㉖
A converted theatre which is now a hip hop, R&B and Desi mainstay. Buy one get one free on all drinks (including bottles of spirits) make Mondays dangerous, while Fridays play host to the award-winning urban night, No.1 Fridays.

The Music Room

Majestic Hotel Tower (04 501 2534). **Open** midday-3am daily. **Map** p82 C2 ㉗
Home to some impressive touring bands, it plays host to some of the best resident bands in town. With an appreciative crowd and decent food and drinks, it's always a safe bet.

Rock Bottom Café

Regent Palace Hotel (04 396 3888). **Open** midday-3am daily. **Map** p82 D3 ㉘
A mainstay on the local scene thanks to a raucous atmosphere, commercial cover bands and an interior that borrows heavily from '60s and '70s

Rock Bottom Café

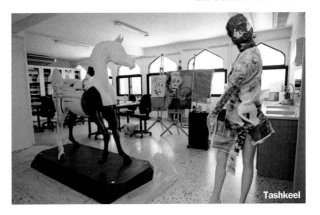

Tashkeel

American culture. It's also home to the popular local drink the Bullfrog (beware the blue tongue the next day), and comes with an in-house shawarma stand.

Submarine

Dhow Palace (04 359 9992). **Open** 6pm-3am daily. **Map** p82 B3 **㉙**

Once the darling of the underground scene, Submarine has lost its way recently. But with an interesting nautical theme, and new promoters pushing everything from techno to reggae, you may just find your groove.

Waxy's

Royal Ascot Hotel (04 352 0900). **Open** midday-4pm, 6pm-3am daily. **Map** p82 C3 **㉚**

A Dubai institution, largely thanks to a consistent approach: cheap drinks, cheap food and a non-stop party playlist. The atmosphere can border on bawdy, so don't expect a quiet pint, but their sports coverage is excellent.

Arts & leisure

The Majlis Gallery

Bastakiya, Bur Dubai (04 353 6233, www.themajlisgallery.com). **Open** 10am-6pm Sat-Thur. **Map** p82 D2 **㉛**

A long-running courtyard and series of exhibition rooms showcasing some carefully selected local and international art.

Tashkeel

Bastakiya, (04 336 3313, www.tashkeel.org). **Open** 10am-8pm Sat-Thur. **Map** p82 D2 **㉜**

A local studio and exhibition space that caters for up-and-coming UAE-based artists. Expect a range of diverse styles and mediums, best to just pop in and see what's on.

Oud Metha

Sights & museums

Al Khor Wildlife Sanctuary

Ras Al Khor industrial area (04 223 2323, www.wildlife.ae). **Open** 9am-4pm Mon-Thur, Sun. **Admission** free. **Map** p83 A6 **㉝**

The country's first site under the Ramsar Convention (committed to conserving wetlands), during winter, it supports more than 20,000 water birds of 67 species and acts as a critical staging ground for migration along the East African-West Asian Flyway. There are three hides open

DUBAI BY AREA

Asha's

Fire & Ice

to the public. The first, Flamingo, is opposite the Emarat garage on Oud Metha Road. From here it's a short walk to the quieter Lagoon sanctuary. Return to Oud Metha Road, then take the left turn to Ras Al Khor, to find the Mangrove hide. For guided tours or to camp here, apply to the Environment Department at Dubai Municipality, forms are available on their website.

Eating & drinking

Asha's

Wafi (04 324 0000). **Open** noon-3pm, 7pm-11pm daily. **$$$**. **Indian**.
Map p83 B6 ㉞
Although pricier than a lot of Indian restaurants in the vicinity, Asha's adds extra twists to bring meals out of the ordinary. Try the sultan puri kebabs or a monaji chicken curry, which comes with chillis, coriander and tomatoes. Round off with a pistachio kulfi.

Betawi Café

4B Street, behind the Ministry of Health (050 226 0889). **Open** noon-midnight daily. **$**. **South-East Asian**.
Map p82 C3 ㉟
Time Out's Budget Restaurant of the Year, this Indonesian treasure in

Karama is an absolute find. Although a little hidden, it's a secret favourite of many top chefs in the city for the wholesome ingredients and delicious flavours. Order piles of satay covered in homemade sauce or try opar ayam – chicken braised in coconut broth.

Chutney's

Mövenpick hotel (04 310 4340). **Open** noon-3pm, 7pm-11.30pm daily. **$$**.
Indian. **Map** p83 B5 ㊱
A quirky Indian haunt that allows you to close curtains around your table for an ultra-intimate dining experience. With a small menu full of interesting dishes, Chutney's keeps things simple and stands out among the huge number of restaurants in this area.

Fire & Ice

Raffles (04 324 8888). **Open** 7pm-midnight daily. **$$$**. **Steakhouse**.
Map p83 B6 ㊲
This high-end restaurant was converted to a steakhouse a couple of years ago with medium success. It has a New York loft-feel, with plenty of exposed brick and steel, but with an elegant finish. Everything at Raffles is extremely well presented, steaks here included, but you'll pay a pretty penny for it. Bring the credit card.

Fish Basket

*Opposite Mövenpick Hotel (04 336
7177).* **Open** 1pm-midnight daily. **$$.**
Seafood. Map p83 B5 ⊛
Fish Basket is unlike any other
restaurant, you buy the whole fish
and dictate how you want it served.
It works best if all your dining party
want the same thing, otherwise it can
be expensive. While you wait, tuck
into the fresh Arabic bread and dips.
Their homemade tartare sauce is
worth a whirl.

Khan Murjan

Wafi (04 327 9795). **Open** 10am-
11.30pm daily. **$$. Arabic**. Map p83
B6 ⊛
With its winning blend of authentic
flavours and great atmospheric decor,
Khan Murjan proved a worthy winner
of the award for Best MENA in the
2011 Restaurant Awards. It's located
in a pretty little courtyard in Wafi's
underground souk, so seek it out.

Khazana

Al Nasr Leisureland (04 336 0061).
Open 12.30pm-2.30pm, 7pm-11.30pm
daily. **$$$. Indian**. Map p83 C5 ⊛

Sanjeev Kapoor's Khazana is the
Indian celebrity chef's signature
restaurant in Dubai, and the master's
impeccable touch is apparent in its
every detail. Khazana insists on
smart casual dressing and the air
of propriety pervades throughout.
It's expensive compared to its peers,
but most of the starters and mains
come in generous portions.

Lemongrass

Next to Lamcy Plaza (04 334 2325).
Open noon-11.30pm daily. **$$. Thai**.
Map p83 B5 ⊛
Lemongrass is a decent independent
Thai restaurant which offers classics,
including a worthy tom yum soup and
a tasty Thai green curry. Friendly and
atmospheric, the food's consistently
good for a reasonable price.

Red Lounge

Raffles (04 324 8888). **Open** 6pm-2am
Sun-Wed; 6pm-3am Thur-Sat. **$$. Bar**.
Map p83 B6 ⊛
This kitsch new-ish bar sits near the
apex of the Raffles hotel pyramid,
affording drinkers a decent view over
the city's skyline. Trinkets from Asia

Fish Basket

DUBAI BY AREA

are scattered around, the overriding colour scheme might prove too much for some, but a couple of finely mixed cocktails might change your mind.

Vintage

Wafi (04 324 4100). **Open** 6pm-1.30am Sat-Wed; 4pm-2am Thur-Fri. **$$. Bar**. **Map** p83 B6 ⑬
A full-on wine and cheese bar, Vintage serves up delicious platters of the smelly stuff or cold cuts, and has an exemplary cellar to pair them with. Their comfy couches are places to settle down for the afternoon.

Wox

Grand Hyatt (04 317 2222). **Open** noon-midnight Sat-Wed; noon-1am Thur-Fri. **$$. Asian**. **Map** p83 B6 ⑭
Sure, you don't go to Wox for a long, languid, lazy meal, but you do go there for high quality, affordable Asian fare – you will be out the door within an hour, but you'll be truly satisfied. The complimentary Oolong tea is free flowing, keeping indigestion at bay, after all that rich food.

Shopping

Daiso

Lamcy Plaza (04 335 1532). **Open** 10am-10.30pm Sun-Wed; 10am-11.30pm Thur-Sat. **Map** p83 B5 ⑮
This cut-price Japanese store sells the wonderful (cute ceramics from South Asia), the weird (vomit bags and more) and the wonderfully useless (garden gnomes and the like) – everything is super cheap. A paradise for those who love random junk.

Desert Rose

Wafi (04 324 6782). **Open** 10am-10pm Sat-Wed; 10am-midnight Thur-Fri. **Map** p83 B6 ⑯
A multi-brand women's boutique that stocks lesser-known labels like Tadashi, Alice & Trixie, Carolee, Pura Lopez, What Comes Around Goes Around and One Grey Day.

Ginger & Lace

Wafi (04 324 5699). **Open** 10am-10pm Sat-Wed; 10am-midnight Thur-Fri. **Map** p83 B6 ⑰
Sugar pink walls and ornate hanging rails set the tone in this quirky, girly boutique, which stocks everything from Betsey Johnson to Wheels & Doll Baby. There's also another branch at Ibn Battuta Mall near Jebel Ali.

Holy Trinity Thrift Store

Holy Trinity Church, Oud Metha Road (04 337 4947). **Open** 10.30am-1pm Thur-Sun; 5pm-7pm Wed. **Map** p83 C5 ⑱
This store is worth a mention as it's one of the few charity stores in the UAE – run by the church, you'll find all sorts of second-hand clothes and household items in here. You can also donate items to the store.

Khan Murjan Souk

Wafi (04 324 4100). **Open** 10am-10pm Sat-Wed; 10am-midnight Thur-Fri. **Map** p83 B6 ⑲
This Arabian-style souk in Wafi Mall has a surprisingly genuine ambience, considering it's effectively brand new. A posh place to pick up trinkets if the real souks are too hot or dirty for you. It's home to *Time Out* Dubai's Middle Eastern Restaurant of the Year 2011 award-winner of the same name, Khan Murjan (see p.75).

Malene Birger

Wafi (04 324 0893). **Open** 10am-10pm Sat-Wed; 10am-midnight Thur-Fri. **Map** p83 B6 ⑳
This Danish designer's boutique is heaven for a grown-up fashionista – Michelle Monaghan and Kate Bosworth are celebrity fans.

Salam Studio

Wafi (04 704 8484). **Open** 10am-10pm Sat-Wed; 10am-midnight Thur-Fri. **Map** p83 B6 ㉑
Unbeatable prices and a vast range of products make this store the most

Ginger & Lace

reliable photography specialist in Dubai. There's no need to trawl the internet for that obscure tripod anymore, as you can bet your bottom dirham that it will be nestling somewhere in the corner of this large general store.

Tigerlily

Wafi (04 324 8088). **Open** 10am-10pm Sat-Wed; 10am-midnight Thur-Fri. **Map** p83 B6 ⑫

Shopping here is a true delight. Draping rails filled with flowing, feminine dresses vie for your attention, while kitsch accessories compete to catch your eye. Look out for pieces by UK favourite Julien MacDonald as well as Australia's hottest exports Sass & Bide.

Nightlife

Chi @ The Lodge

Al Nasr Leisureland (04 337 9470). **Open** 9pm-3am daily. **Map** p83 C5 ⑬

Popular four-roomed club, with a 2,000 capacity al fresco 'garden' at the centre, which has played host to Groove Armada, Armin Van Buuren and more. The club has just opened a brand new pub, imaginatively titled Cheers, with a resident cover band and drink deals.

People by Crystal

Raffles Dubai (04 342 8888). **Open** 10pm-3am daily. **Map** p83 B6 ⑭

Commercial clubbing with a strong Lebanese following. The music is loud, the views are impressive and the decor is stunning, if a little OTT. It can get very busy at weekends, so either come early or make sure your name is on the list. There's also often a dress code, so look smart.

Arts & leisure

Al Nasr Leisureland Ice Rink

Oud Metha, (04 337 1234, www. alnasrll.com). **Open** 9am-midnight daily. **Map** p83 C5 ⑮

This small but handy ice rink hosts casual skating, as well as ice hockey and figure skating at the old fashioned Al Nasr Leisureland centre. One of Dubai's less busy rinks, it's a good place for those a bit like Bambi on ice. Casual skating costs Dhs25 for two hours, plus Dhs10 for skate hire.

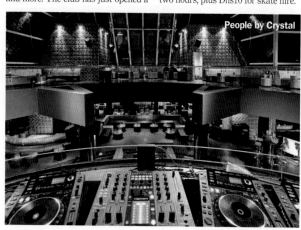
People by Crystal

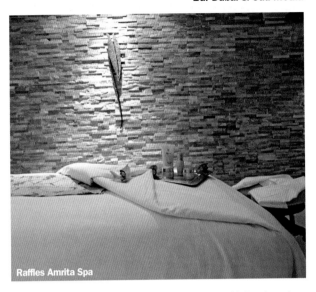

Raffles Amrita Spa

Al Nasr Leisureland Tennis Courts

Oud Metha (04 337 1234, www.alnasrll. com). **Open** 6am-11pm daily. **Map** p83 C5 **56**
Al Nasr also has four standard tennis courts (as well as one for coaching and a mini-sized court). You can book the floodlit courts by calling that day.

Grand Spa

Grand Hyatt Dubai, Oud Metha, (04 317 2333, www.dubai.grand.hyatt). **Open** 9am-9pm daily. **Map** p83 B6 **57**
This is a tasteful candlelit spa, which stocks New York brands June Jacobs and Bella Lucce. It's around Dhs370 for a facial, but their massages are truly heavenly.

Lama Tours

Al Sayegh Building, Oud Metha Road (04 334 4330, www.lama.ae). **Open** 9am-9pm daily. **Map** p83 C5 **58**
Lama Tours will pick you up and ferry you over to the Flamingo Beach

Resort in Umm Al Quwain and set you loose in the mangroves to spear crabs and squids. The resort will then cook your kill for you. Unique and well worth booking.

Monty's Rowing School

Al Boom Tourist Village (050 738 0910, www.montysrowingschool.com). **Open** 5am-10am, 4pm-7.30pm daily. **Map** p83 A6 **59**
Learn to row on the picturesque Dubai Creek. All ages and abilities are welcome. Call for more details.

Raffles Amrita Spa

Raffles Dubai, Oud Metha, (04 314 9869, www.dubai.raffles.com). **Open** 9am-9pm daily. **Map** p83 B6 **60**
This superior luxury spa is one of the city's best. Feel at one with the outdoors in the attached garden and outside pool. Their body wraps are consistently some of the most sought after in Dubai and are a perfect reviver after a night out. Pure bliss.

Sheikh Zayed Road

DIFC, Downtown & Sheikh Zayed Road

Sheikh Zayed Road is the main artery of Dubai, pumping traffic round the city and keeping it moving. Its main focus used to be the be the area now known as Trade Centre and what has evolved into Dubai International Financial Centre (DIFC). But with the building of Old Town and Downtown (the names are almost interchangeable), which are the surrounding developments at the bottom of the world's tallest building Burj Khalifa, this emphasis has moved somewhat.

DIFC has now expanded to include a high-end selection of boutiques, art galleries, restaurants and bars to appease its financial clientele and here you'll also find the recently opened Le Petite Maison (see p97), named *Time Out Dubai*'s Best Newcomer restaurant in 2011. However, the more major arrival of an entirely new area of Dubai under the shadow of the Burj Khalifa has completely redefined the city, creating more of a 'centre' than it has ever had before. The largest mall in the world anchors this feeling, located alongside the Dubai Fountains attraction and a whole slew of restaurants and bars with lake and Burj views in the malls, hotels and Souk Al Bahar complex. Emaar Boulevard is the ring road that encircles the new development and wide pavements are starting to foster little cafés, while the five-star hotels offer a holiday, right at the centre of Dubai.

Back on Sheikh Zayed Road, this multi-lane highway offers the quickest connection to New Dubai – based round TECOM, Media City, Dubai Marina and the Palm. You'll see the new metro line running alongside the road, it offers a much cheaper (but slower) alternative to taxis (see p177), but also has some of the best views of the expanding city, thanks to its elevated position.

DIFC

Eating & drinking

Al Nafoorah
Jumeirah Emirates Towers (04 310 8088). **Open** 12.30pm-4pm, 8pm-midnight daily. **$$$**. **Middle Eastern**. **Map** p99 E4 ➊
One of the city's finest Arabic restaurants, Sheikh Mohammed bin Rashid Al Maktoum is an occasional visitor, think elegant banquets of mezze, grilled dishes and traditional umm ali for dessert. If you want to sample the local cuisine in style, look no further.

The Agency
Jumeirah Emirates Towers (04 319 8088). **Open** 7pm-10.30pm daily; 12.30pm-2pm Sun-Thur. **$$$**. **Bar**. **Map** p99 E4 ➋
Having recently relocated within the Emirates Towers complex, The Agency now finds itself adjacent to the popular Rib Room in the hotel lobby. Thankfully, for fans of the popular wine bar and its sister in the Madinat Jumeirah, the move works. With a snack menu as varied as its wine list, it's a winner.

Caramel
Building 3, DIFC (04 425 6677, www.caramelgroup.com). **Open** 11am-2am daily. **$$**. **Bar**. **Map** p99 D4 ➌
Caramel's a sophisticated, trendy low-lit restaurant/lounge with a lovely alfresco area that's as happy catering to the nearby banking sector as it is the cool and classy fashionistas in town. Good music, great food and impressive drinks.

The Ivy
Jumeirah Emirates Towers (04 319 8767). **Open** noon-3.30pm; 6pm-11pm daily. **$$$**. **British**. **Map** p99 E4 ➍
Dubai's most recent European chain to stake a claim in the Middle East is the iconic Ivy. A feel for the original makes this smart but informal restaurant a future favourite. Modern European dishes keep things simple, but delicious.

La Petite Maison
Gate Village (04 439 0505). **Open** noon-3pm Sun-Sat; 7pm-11pm Sun-Sat. **$$$**. **French**. **Map** p99 D4 ➎
La Petite Maison, the cosy restaurant that first sprung up in Nice back in 1988, has found a perfect home in DIFC, tucked away amid art galleries and boutique stores. Guests approach its shuttered façade via a leafy courtyard rather than through a hotel lobby. The restaurant's interior takes the form of a high-end French bistro (a near-carbon copy of the Mayfair venue) and the food follows suit.

Rib Room
Jumeirah Emirates Towers (04 319 8088). **Open** 7pm-10.30pm daily; 12.30pm-2pm Sun-Thur. **$$$**. **Steakhouse**. **Map** p99 E4 ➏
Succulent cuts abound at this re-launched high-end steakhouse. The menu also caters for those not so keen on cow, with diabetic and veggie options. Smart leather chairs, glass-encased wine cellar and an intimate space used well.

Tokyo@The Towers
Jumeirah Emirates Towers (04 319 8088). **Open** noon-3pm, 7pm-midnight Sun-Thur; 1pm-4pm, 7pm-midnight Fri-Sat. **$$$**. **Japanese**. **Map** p99 D4 ➐

Caramel p97

Dubai Fountains p102

DIFC, Downtown & SZR

JUMEIRAH 2

Choithram Supermarket

AL WASL RD (D 92 RD)

AL WASL RD (D 92 RD)

Medcare Hospital

AL HADIQA ST

Safa Park 84

AL WASL

61 63 64 65 66 67 81 85 90

Interchange 2 (Exit 47)

Salik H

Maza Centr

SHEIKH ZAYED ROAD (E-11)

Oasis Centre

72

Business Bay

DOWNTOW BURJ KHAL

AL QUOZ

MEYDAN ROAD

46

HAJAR ROAD

BUSINESS BAY

0   1 km
0   1000 yds

© Copyright Time Out Group 2011

Candylicious p105

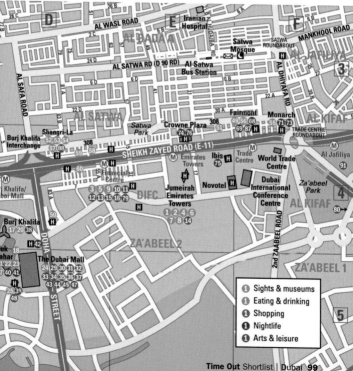

Map labels:

AL WASL ROAD

AL BADA'A

Iranian Hospital

Satwa Mosque

SATWA ROUNDABOUT

MANKHOOL ROAD

AL SATWA RD (D 90 RD)

Al Satwa Bus Station

AL DHIYAFA RD

W JAFILIYA

3

AL SAFA ROAD

AL SATWA

Satwa Park

Fairmont

Monarch

AL KIFAF

Shangri-La

Crowne Plaza

308

Burj Khalifa Interchange

308

SHEIKH ZAYED ROAD (E-11)

TRADE CENTRE ROUNDABOUT

Emirates Towers

Ibis

Trade Centre

World Trade Centre

Al Jafiliya

Financial Centre

DIFC

Jumeirah Emirates Towers

Novotel

Dubai International Conference Centre

Za'abeel Park

AL KIFAF

Burj Khalifa

ZA'ABEEL 2

ZA'ABEEL 1

The Dubai Mall

DOHA STREET

2nd ZA'ABEEL ROAD

ZA'ABEEL 5

- 1 Sights & museums
- 1 Eating & drinking
- 1 Shopping
- 1 Nightlife
- 1 Arts & leisure

With authentic sunken tables, always entertaining live teppanyaki grills and bamboo everywhere, Tokyo@ The Towers feels like a restaurant you might actually come across in its namesake city (except for most of the staff not being Japanese, that is). The food is consistent – and worth it.

Vu's

Jumeirah Emirates Towers (04 319 8088). Open 6pm-3am daily. **$$**. **Bar**. **Map** p99 E4 **8**

Though rumour has it this place at the top of the Emirates Towers Hotel – above the restaurant of the same name – is to undergo a makeover, one thing that's certain to remain the same is the view – the main reason to pay a visit to this 51st floor spot via a glass elevator. Perfect for gawping out over Satwa and Jumeirah, and straight over to the Gulf, be sure to sample some of the vertiginous bar's excellent (and rather strong) cocktails.

Zuma

Building 6, DIFC (04 425 5660, www. zumarestaurant.com). Open 6pm-3am daily. **$$$**. **Japanese**. **Map** p99 D4 **9**

One of the best looking bars in Dubai, Zuma has a music policy and food menu to match. The music is a toe-tapping mix of nu-disco and classic house and builds perfectly as the night gets busier, while the Japanese-accented food comes in small but sublime portions.

Shopping

Bespoke Tailors

Basement area, Dubai International Financial Centre (04 363 7237). **Open** 10am-8pm daily. **Map** p99 E4 **10**

This tailor's is a little more expensive than those you'd find in Satwa or Bur Dubai, but because of that you're ensured quality and a well-cut suit that fits you to a tee. The service from the Parmar family is excellent. And they can turn suits round quickly.

Arts & leisure

ArtSpace

Gate Village 3, DIFC. (04 323 0820, www.artspace-dubai.com). **Open** 10am-8.30pm daily. **Map** p99 E4 **11**

A contemporary gallery that focuses on Middle Eastern art, exhibitions change every three weeks or so.

The Empty Quarter

Gate Village 2, DIFC (04 323 1210, www.theemptyquarter.com). **Open** 9am-10pm Sat-Thur, 3pm-10pm Fri. **Map** p99 D4 **12**

Dubai's only gallery dedicated solely to photography, this gallery boasts an alterable space and library, and has featured some impressively wide-ranging exhibitions.

Farjam Collection Gallery

Gate Village 4, DIFC (04 323 0303, www.farjamcollection.com). **Open** 10am-8pm daily. **Map** p99 D4 **13**

The not-for-profit gallery holds a series of regular educational programmes for children and also offers free audio tours of this impressive private collection of Middle Eastern works.

Talise Spa and Wellness Clinic

Jumeirah Emirates Towers (04 319 8181). **Open** 9am-10pm daily. **Map** p99 E4 **14**

Zuma

The best of the brunch

Get the lowdown on this popular Friday institution.

While the aftermaths of these have, on occasion, made UK tabloid headlines in the past, brunches are part of the recreational landscape for expatriates and holidaymakers in the UAE. Unlike in the UK, brunch in Dubai normally kicks off around midday on a Friday, lasting three or four hours (depending on the venue) and including generous buffet spreads and unlimited alcohol (again, the beverage choice depends on venue and the tier brunch you've opted for). Whether you've got your sights set on a lavish, champagne and caviar affair in one of Dubai's most opulent five-star hotels, or a more flip flop-friendly knees up in one of the city's lively pubs, there are over 100 different brunches to choose from. Recently, the city's eateries have seized upon the idea of evening brunches on Friday nights and increasingly are offering similar deals on Saturdays. Though, with the later being the last day of the weekend in the UAE, proceedings are usually a little more subdued in the knowledge everyone will be off to work first thing the next morning.

At the top end of the brunching spectrum, such as the Al Qasr brunch at the five-star hotel in Jumeirah, brunchers are spoilt for choice in every direction they look, with everything from freshly made sushi to roast dinners, a barbecue station and a whole room filled with nothing but chocolate desserts. And it's not just about the food, there's a cigar station where you'll find a chap hand-rolling the hours away, cocktail stations and champagne top-ups before you've even drained half your glass. It's not cheap at Dhs495 a pop, but definitely worth trying once.

There are also plenty of more reasonable brunches to enjoy, particularly if you opt for soft drinks only. An affordable deal that includes unlimited house wine and beer will usually cost Dhs200 upwards. For Dhs215, Dusit Thani Dubai allows you access to a buffet of Chinese, Thai, British and American fare, and all the house drinks you can manage.

▪ Dusit Thani Dubai, (04 343 3333).

▪ Al Qasr Hotel (04 366 6730).

DUBAI BY AREA

For a spot of urban tranquility, try the chakra balancing treatment, which involves essential oil blends and crystals. Facials start from Dhs495.

Urban Male Lounge

Building 2, Gate 2, DIFC (04 425 0350). **Open** 10am-9pm Sat-Thur; noon-9pm Fri. **Map** p99 D4 ⑮
This modern retreat has Dubai's males checking in for their grooming sessions in droves.

XVA Gallery

Building 7, Gate Village, DIFC (04 358 5117). **Open** 11am-8pm Sun-Thur; 4pm-8pm Sat. **Map** p99 E4 ⑯
The previous Bastakiya stalwarts have opened a second, very sleek exhibition space in DIFC, which is fast becoming a hot spot for modern art and photography exhibitions.

XVA Gallery

Downtown

Sights & museums

Burj Khalifa

Downtown Dubai, 1 Emaar Boulevard (04 888 8124, www.burjkhalifa.ae). **Open** 10am-midnight daily. Admission Dhs100 online, Dhs400 on the day. **Map** p99 D4 ⑰
Construction on the Burj Khalifa began way back in 2004 and today, the world's tallest tower stands at 828 metres high, putting Dubai well and truly on the world map. The 160-floor building is home to the famous Armani Hotel, the world's highest swimming pool and restaurant, and the world's highest observation deck (on a man-made structure), on level 124. Getting up there is half the fun, as the high-speed elevators put on a great show as they make their way up at speeds of 10 metres per second. Views from the deck are spectacular, but you'll also be fascinated by the interactive displays that show you what Dubai looked like decades ago.

Dubai Fountains

Dubai Mall/Souk al Bahar, Downtown. **Map** p99 D5 ⑱
When Dubai builds fountains it really builds fountains, these babies are the tallest in the world and designed by the team behind the world famous jets at the Bellagio in Las Vegas. Set to music, the fountains 'dance' in time to the pieces which go off once every 20 minutes in the afternoon and evening. For the best view, go for a meal at one of the many lakeside restaurants in The Dubai Mall or the (licensed) Souk Al Bahar complex.

Eating & drinking

Al Samadi Cafe and Sweet Shop

The Boulevard, Old Town, Burj Khalifa (04 432 9520). **Open** 11am-midnight daily. **$. Café. Map** p98 C4 ⑲
Arabic sweets are the name of the game here, at this elegant, art deco-style Franco-Lebanese café. Dark wooden furniture and plates of goodies under glass domes help carry you away on a sugar high, with pastries to pistachio-laden baklava.

At.mosphere

Burj Khalifa, Al Doha Street, Downtown (04 888 3828). **Open** noon-2am daily. **$$$$**. **Steakhouse**. Map p99 D4 ⑳

Positioned 122 floors up, this is officially the tallest restaurant in the world and one that is refreshingly gimmick free. Split between a bar lounge (minimum spend Dhs200 per person) and a steakhouse restaurant, At.mosphere's small-ish menu is actually pretty good. Steaks are cooked in a Spanish 'josper' charcoal oven which flames them in minutes.

Baker & Spice

Souk Al Bahar (04 425 2240). **Open** 8am-11.30pm daily. **$$**. **Café**. Map p99 D5 ㉑

There are some brilliant dishes on offer at the Dubai incarnation of this British wholefoods café. A great place to hit at the weekends, but it's not on the cheap side.

Bice Mare

Souk Al Bahar (04 423 0982). **Open** noon-midnight daily. **$$**. **Seafood**. Map p99 D5 ㉒

Bice Mare

The venue is fantastic – especially the outdoor terrace overlooking the Dubai Fountains – and the interior is quintessentially Italian (think crisp white table clothes, black and white photos adorning the walls, glinting glassware), but service can be a little hit-and-miss.

Mango Tree

Souk Al Bahar (04 426 7313). **Open** 12.30pm-midnight daily. **$$**. **Thai**. Map p99 D5 ㉓

Thai restaurant with a great reputation and a spectacular view, but you'll need to book a table if you want a seat on the terrace or the lively bar area – the back room is a bit of a no man's land of service. Stay away from the lobster and crab dishes unless you want to flex the plastic.

More

The Dubai Mall (04 339 8934). **Open** 10am-10pm Sat-Wed; 10am-midnight Thur-Fri. **Café**. Map p99 D5 ㉔

Although this local chain of cafés can be found now at most malls, you'd be hard pushed to beat the views from this one at The Dubai Mall. Watch the fountains as you tuck into a croissant, burgers or South African dishes.

Neos

The Address Downtown (04 436 8880). Open 7pm-2.30am daily. **$$**. **Bar**. Map p99 D5 ㉕

All locals take visitors to Neos – well they should anyway, to experience a view of Dubai from 63 floors up. Sleek, black marble and floor-to-ceiling windows never fail to impress and neither does the cocktail list. A real treat for visitors.

Nezesaussi

Al Manzil Hotel (04 428 5888). **Open** 6pm-2am Sun-Thur; noon-2am Fri-Sat. **$$**. **Pub**. Map p98 C5 ㉖

Ignore the unpronounceable name and get stuck into one of their pies at this lively expat bar that, despite its

DUBAI BY AREA

location, leaves all pretension at the door. Great for a midweek meal.

The Rivington Grill
Souk Al Bahar (04 423 0903). **Open** noon-11pm daily. **$$. British**. Map p99 D5 ㉗

The Dubai outpost of the London gastropub has found a fond home among the city's stomachs – with its line in pies, roast dinners and Yorkshire pudding a special favourite. Sleek, stylish and with a great view, the restaurant also doesn't mind people whiling away the hours with a pint of ale and a newspaper.

Thiptara
The Palace (04 428 7888). **Open** 7pm-midnight daily. **$$$. Thai**. Map p99 D5 ㉘

For high-end Thai food look no further. Thiptara sparkles with romantic possibilities and if you're in Dubai on honeymoon, then this place is a must. Although all the usual Thai staples are in place, give the duck curry with lychees a whirl.

Shopping

The Art Source Gallery
The Dubai Mall, Downtown Burj Khalifa (04 339 8399, www. theartsource97.com). **Open** 10am-10pm Sun-Thu; 10am-midnight Fri-Sat. **Map** p99 D5 ㉙

Gallery and store showcasing a collection of artworks, accessories, metal sculptures and more. They also offer framing services if you find that perfect print.

Bloomingdale's
The Dubai Mall (04 350 5333). **Open** 10am-10pm Sat-Wed; 10am-midnight Thur-Fri. **Map** p99 D5 ㉚

The fact that this iconic New York department store chose to open its only other branch in Dubai is a testament to how much we like shopping here. The two-part store has contemporary clothing, designer wares, home goods and even a separate Museum of Modern Arts section from New York. Oh, and there's a Magnolia Bakery selling delectable cupcakes – lush.

Bloomingdale's

Book World by Kinokuniya

The Dubai Mall (04 434 0111). **Open** 10am-10pm Sat-Wed; 10am-midnight Thur-Fri. **Map** p99 D5 ❸❶

You could genuinely lose a tour bus of people in this Japanese bookstore. Selling a great range of, well, everything, our only complaint is that it doesn't sell a single newspaper. Head to café, which has a great view.

Candylicious

The Dubai Mall (04 330 8700). **Open** 10am-10pm Sat-Wed; 10am-midnight Thur-Fri. **Map** p99 D5 ❸❷

Head here on a Friday night and you will be trampled – this Willy Wonka-style candy haven sells everything from giant Hershey's pillows to gourmet chocolates and fizzing lollipops. Truly an assault on the senses (particularly on taste).

Fashion Avenue

The Dubai Mall (04 362 7500). **Open** 10am-10pm Sat-Wed; 10am-midnight Thur-Fri. **Map** p99 D5 ❸❸

Alexander McQueen, Marni, Elie Saab, Chloé and more line this ultra luxurious part of The Dubai Mall – as good for people watching as it is for shopping. Plonk yourself down on one of the plush sofas and watch minted locals, football players and glamorous tourists all brush shoulders, spending up a designer storm.

Galeries Lafayette

The Dubai Mall (04 339 9933). **Open** 10am-10pm Sat-Wed; 10am-midnight Thur-Fri. **Map** p99 D5 ❸❹

This Parisian department store, founded in the 1890s, opened its Dubai branch to much fanfare in 2009. The 20,000 square feet of space is crammed with a gourmet supermarket and, of course, fashion.

Manolo Blahnik

The Dubai Mall (04 339 8122). **Open** 10am-10pm Sat-Wed; 10am-midnight Thur-Fri. **Map** p99 D5 ❸❺

Love shoes? Look no further. Blahnik's first store to open in the Middle East has become a haven for heel-lovers. It's beautiful window displays attract even the hardiest soul, like moths to a flame.

Symphony

The Dubai Mall (04 330 8050). **Open** 10am-10pm Sat-Wed; 10am-midnight Thur-Fri. **Map** p99 D5 ❸❻

A cute, girly independent boutique selling a range of brands like Charlotte Olympia and Prabal Gurung.

Tom Ford

The Dubai Mall (04 330 8300). **Open** 10am-10pm Sat-Wed; 10am-midnight Thur-Fri. **Map** p99 D5 ❸❼

This masculine, slick store is worth a look just for the design. Tom Ford is a huge hit with Emirati men, so much so that he produced a range of colognes to suit this market.

Nightlife

Armani Prive

Armani Hotel Dubai, Burj Khalifa (04 888 3308, www.armanihotels.com). **Open** 10pm-3am daily. **Map** p99 D4 ❸❽

From the squash-court sized plasma screen that dominates one wall, to the pricey-even-for-Dubai drinks menu, everything in Armani screams opulence and that goes for the clientele as well. Weekends are packed, so bring a credit card and settle down for some excellent people-watching.

Calabar

The Address Downtown (04 436 8888, www.theaddress.com). **Open** 6pm-3am daily. **Map** p99 D5 ❸❾

Hip hop and house fans are well catered for, but if you're looking for some soul, funk and broken beat then weekly night Bar Rumba at Calabar is your best bet. Located near the base of the Burj Khalifa, it comes with impressive views over the Dubai Fountains and a great terrace.

Karma Kafe

Souk Al Bahar (04 423 0909, www. karma-kafe.com). **Open** 6pm-1am Sun-Wed; midday-4pm, 6pm-2am Thur-Sat. **Map** p99 D5 ⑩

Taking inspiration from ever popular Buddha Bar, Karma Kafe offers award-winning international fare (the sushi is particularly good here), outstanding cocktails and one of the best world-music playlists in the city, with regular international guests.

Left Bank

Souk Al Bahar (04 368 4501, www. soukalbahar.ae). **Open** 6pm-2am daily. **Map** p99 D5 ⑪

See Madinat Jumeirah p137.

Republique

The Address, Dubai Mall (050 488 0876, www.clubrepublique.com). **Open** 10pm-3am Mon-Sun. **Map** p99 D4 ⑫

Dubai's latest club to open in 2011, Republique is looking to cater to the older, and alternative audience. The music is a mish-mash of '80s and '90s classics (and not so classics). The small bar/club is kitted out with a fierce soundsystem and can generate a full on party atmosphere but it needs a while yet to warm up to make a dent on the city's music scene.

Arts & leisure

Dubai Aquarium

The Dubai Mall, Al Doha street (04 448 5200 **Open** 10am-10pm Sun-Wed, 10am-midnight Thur-Sat. **Map** p99 D5 ⑬

Housing over 33,000 aquatic animals and over 140 species plus over 400 tiger sharks and the largest collection of sand tiger sharks in the world. There's a 48 metre walk through tunnel and they also offer shark dives and feeding sessions daily (starting from Dhs100 although you'll need a PADI license). Dhs50 per person for the Underwater Zoo.

Dubai Ice Rink

The Dubai Mall, Downtown Burj Khalifa, (04 437 3111, www. dubaiicerink.com). **Open** 10am-midnight Sun-Wed; 11.15am-midnight Thur-Sat. **Map** p99 D5 ⑭

This Olympic-sized rink facilitates social skating, school visits, private parties and all manner of ice-related revelry. Public sessions usually take place in the mornings and resume in the afternoon, while private lessons take place around midday. Dhs50-Dhs75 (includes skate hire).

Nivea Haus

The Dubai Mall, Downtown Burj Khalifa (04 434 0777, www.en.nivea-me.com). **Open** 10am-10pm daily. **Map** p99 D5 ⑮

Stop off for skin/hair analysis, manis/pedis, waxing, hair styling, make-up and massage, all using Nivea products. For a spa, this one is pretty reasonable if you're after functional and not pampering. Facials from only around Dhs140.

The Pavilion

Emaar Boulevard, Downtown Dubai (04 447 7025). **Open** 10am-midnight daily. **Map** p98 C5 ⑯

This is the hippest art spot of the moment. The minimalist earthy tones create a blank canvas for your mind and perfect place to hang out enjoy a coffee, go to a workshop or put on an exhibition. Check out the amazing wicker sculpture in the garden too – you can't miss it.

Reel Cinemas

Dubai Mall (04 449 1988, www. reelcinemas.ae). **Open** 10am-midnight daily. **Map** p99 D5 ⑰

With 22 screens showing most of the latest blockbusters, plus swish VIP Platinum Movie Suites, where you can wait in a VIP room before your film and sit in extra large chairs during the movie that recline. Order food from a waiter by pressing a button

The Pavillion

on your table. Prices vary by screen. Also check the Picturehouse next door, which despite being in a mall, is Dubai's only art-house cinema.

The Spa at The Address
The Address, Downtown Dubai (04 436 8888, www.theaddress.com). **Open** 9am-9pm Sat-Tue; 9am-10pm Wed-Fri. **Map** p99 D5 ❹❽
Check into this luxe spa for the city's best views of the Dubai fountains. Seriously luxurious for those who want a real treat of an afternoon. Also check out the hotel's tiered infinity pool from which you can people watch the crowds at Dubai Mall. Five star facials start rom Dhs475.

Sheikh Zayed Road

Eating & drinking

The Cigar Bar
The Fairmont (04 311 8316). **Open** 7pm-2am daily. **$$. Bar. Map** p99 F3 ❹❾
Nestled in the corner next to The Fairmont Dubai's Cin Cin wine bar, this stogie spot is liberally scattered with oversized leather sofas and armchairs, along with a handful of

cigar and whiskey connoisseurs. The atmosphere is more relaxed than that of its neighbour – which draws a younger crowd and can, as a result, feel something of a meat market – making it ideal for quiet drinks.

Double Decker
Al Marooj Rotana (04 321 1111). **Open** noon-3am daily. **Map** p99 D4 ❺⓿
Double Decker is a bar themed around London transport and celebrates everything that's great about the British capital. From the grandiose coats of armour adorning the walls to the hordes of sunburnt punters parading around, it's a home away from home for Brits in Dubai.

Fibber Magee's
Behind Crowne Plaza hotel (04 332 2400). **Open** 8am-1am daily. **$. Pub. Map** p99 E3 ❺❶
One of Dubai's longest-standing Irish-themed pub, Fibber Magee's is a perennial favourite thanks to its casual atmosphere, weekly pub quiz and stellar grub. There's little a homesick expat can't find here to remind them of the bars they've left behind, from pints of ale to the unintentionally-retro upholstery and old school sticky floor.

DUBAI BY AREA

Hoi An

Shangri-La (04 405 2703). **Open**
7pm-midnight daily. **$$$**. **Asian**. Map
p99 D4 ⑫

This is an understated treasure of a
Vietnamese restaurant. A drawing
room like vibe pervades the quiet
atmosphere and it's a good sign that
the restaurant is regularly booked out
even on weeknights, so you're better
off booking ahead.

iKandy

Shangri-La, (04 343 8888). **Open** 6pm-
2am daily. **$$**. **Bar**. Map p99 D4 ⑬

A funky poolside spot that draws a
fashionable crowd, don't be deterred
by the less-than-glamorous sounding
location (it's on top of the Shangri-
La hotel's car park), because there's
much to love about this al-fresco spot.
Unpretentious, laid-back, and just the
right size, you could do a lot worse
than a night out with friends here.

Marrakesh

Shangri-La (04 405 2703). **Open** 7pm-
1am Sat-Thur. **$$**. **Middle Eastern**.
Map p99 D4 ⑭

Marrakesh does refined and
elegant dining effortlessly. From
the immaculate service, down to its
accomplished and authentic Moroccan
cuisine, there is a fluidity to the
whole dining experience. The elegant
Moorish arches, twinkling lanterns
and decorative tiling evoke a tranquil
and sophisticated ambience, but don't
exactly shout 'Arabian Nights'.

Okku

The Monarch (04 501 8777). **Open**
7pm-2am daily. **$$$**. **Japanese**.
Map p99 F3 ⑮

Not one to sit on its laurels as a pretty
place for pretty people to sit, drink,
nibble on sushi and absorb attention,
Chef Hugh Gardiner has diligently
fine-tuned the modern Japanese menu
at Okku, ensuring the food lives up
to – if not surpasses the shimmering,
glittering environs.

Ruth's Chris Steakhouse

The Fairmont (04 501 8666). **Open**
noon-2.30pm; 6pm-11.30pm Sat-
Wed; 6pm-midnight Thur-Fri. **$$$**.
Steakhouse. Map p99 F3 ⑯

Proud of its 45-year-old American
heritage, the chain has restaurants in
more than 32 US states. Far from
being stereotypically brash and
boisterous, it takes the best bits of
American hospitality (first-class
service, a lively vibe), then adds sleek,
modern décor and sinfully tasty food
for a dining experience that ticks all
the boxes. Makes Uncle Sam proud.

Shang Palace

Shangri-La (04 343 8888). **Open**
12.30-2.30pm; 7pm-11.30pm daily. **$$**.
Chinese. Map p99 D4 ⑰

While the food's not especially
exceptional at this traditional Chinese
spot, the service certainly sets it apart
– order a tea and you'll get a Kung Fu
like pouring performance; ask for the
best dishes in the house and you'll get
the entire breadth of Chinese cuisine.

Okku

Teatro

Towers Rotana (04 343 8000). **Open** 4pm-11.30pm daily. **$$**. **International**. Map p99 D4 ⑱

International eatery with a dazzling array of dishes which means there's something for everyone. Although it has a great view of Sheikh Zayed Road it doesn't use it to its best advantage, but still it's a popular local choice.

Zaatar W Zeit

Near Shangri-La hotel (600 522 231). **Open** 24 hours. **$**. **Middle Eastern**. Map p99 D4 ⑲

The buzzy, funky atmosphere and friendly service here lends itself best to groups of friends and casual late-night snacks. Zaatar W Zeit specialises in saj – Lebanese pizza made with flatbread served piping hot from the oven and usually dripping in gooey cheese.

Zaroob

Jumeirah Tower, Sheikh Zayed Road (04 327 6060). **Open** 24 hours. **$**. **Middle Eastern**. Map p99 D4 ⑳

This new Levant street food joint is certainly something different. With exposed concrete floors and corrugated iron walls (each adorned with graffiti and stencils of Arabic icons, such as singer Om Kalthoum), the interiors ooze edge and feel genuinely eclectic, rather than staged.

Shopping

Adventure HQ

Times Square, Sheikh Zayed Road (04 341 8020). **Open** 10am-10pm Sat-Wed; 10am-midnight Thur-Sat. **Map** p98 A4 ㉑

This huge adventure goods store sells everything an intrepid type could ever need and there's even an in-store obstacle course, climbing wall and 'chill' room where you can experience extreme temperatures. Only in Dubai! For all those out of town camping trips, head here to stock up.

At.mosphere

The world's highest restaurant is a must-do.

Unless you've been living in a cave, you'll have likely heard of Dubai's Burj Khalifa, the world's tallest building. This year, the record-breaking structure scored another coup with the opening of At.mosphere, which, perched on the 122nd floor, became the world's highest restaurant after opening in January. This fact alone sent the media into a frenzy, and once again all eyes were on Dubai. Here, it isn't just about the view – that's what the At the Top viewing gallery, located a couple of floors above, is for. This venue is all about the food, and though you will certainly find yourself parting with a handsome sum to enjoy it, enjoy it you will.

At.mosphere's Grill and Lounge are two totally different concepts. The menu in the main restaurant – The Grill – focuses on seasonal products, with the starters and vegetarian dishes changing every three months. The grill can accommodate 80 guests and features a private dining room and chef's table for 12 people. The Lounge, meanwhile, is a more laid-back, casual affair, serving a tapas style menu – perfect for anyone wanting to eat at At.mosphere, but who can't get a table in the main restaurant. The lounge can seat 135 people (there's also a private area that can accommodate 35 guests), and features an in-house DJ. The lounge (open until 2am) also serves afternoon tea from 3pm-6pm, Dhs360 with a glass of champagne (04 888 3828).

DUBAI BY AREA

Dubai Garden Centre

Beautybay

Oasis Centre, Sheikh Zayed Road (04 515 4300). **Open** 10am-10pm Sat-Thur; 10am-midnight Fri. **Map** p98 A4 ⑫

This beauty department store sells all the big brands but also features great niche brands like REN and Korean skincare label Erborian.

Dubai Garden Centre

Exit 43, Sheikh Zayed Road (04 340 0006). **Open** 9am-10pm daily. **Map** p98 A4 ⑬

This fantastic store houses BBQs, plants-a-plenty, Dubai 's best coffee roastery (which serves up a killer flat white) and weekly organic food markets. A true renaissance shop.

Gold and Diamond Park

Sheikh Zayed Road **Map** p98 A4 ⑭

This place does exactly what it suggests. A mini retail park selling only gold and glittery things, this is the best place to head for for a unique engagement ring, jewellery or gift, especially if you don't fancy haggling in the souks.

Objekts of Design

Near Noor Islamic Bank Metro Station, Sheikh Zayed Road (04 328 4301).

Open 10am-8pm Sat-Thur; 2pm-8pm Fri. **Map** p98 A4 ⑮

This hidden away furniture store sells good copies of designer furniture – meaning a classic design will cost you Dhs5,000 instead of Dhs50,000. There's also a decent range of African traditional wooden furniture, although it is a little pricey.

OK

Opposite Volkswagen showroom, Sheikh Zayed Road (04 394 6400). **Open** 9am-9pm Sat-Thur, 5pm-10pm Fri. **Map** p98 A4 ⑯

This 40-year-old locally grown furniture store has over 22,000 chair designs on the books and is very affordable. Many of the items look high design but have decidedly high street price tags – prices range from Dhs155-Dhs2,000.

Sun and Sands Outlet Store

Behind Dubai Garden Centre (04 339 7595). **Open** 10am-11pm Sun-Thur; 10am-midnight Fri-Sat. **Map** p98 A4 ⑰

Hidden behind a slip road of Sheikh Zayed Road in the artistic hub warehouse community of Al Quoz, this outlet store sells kettle bells, designer sneakers and more for cheap.

Nightlife

The 400

The Fairmont (04 332 4900, www. the400nightclub.com) **Open** 11pm-3am daily. **Map** p99 F3 ⑥⑧

Cunningly named as it can hold 400 people, The 400 lives up to its lowest common denominator moniker with its music – think big house, electro and R&B remixes, and a crowd that buys (large) bottles of champagne to show off

Cavalli Club

The Fairmont (04 332 9260, www. cavalliclubdubai.com) **Open** 7pm-3am daily. **Map** p99 F3 ⑥⑨

Part restaurant, part club and all glamour, Cavalli is – as the name cunningly suggests – a spin off from Roberto. So expect bored looking models at the bar, high end food and prices to match at this cavernous but impressive venue.

The Fridge

Al Quoz (04 347 7793, www. thefridgedubai.com). **Open** 10am-10pm (show times normally 8pm). **Map** p98 A5 ⑦⓪

A converted warehouse in the middle of Dubai's industrial estate might not seem an obvious choice, but The Fridge's dedication to music means its Monday night gigs are a mainstay on the alternative scene. Expect everything from dueling pianists to Iranian indie.

Gold

The Monarch (04 501 8888, www. themonarchdubai.com) **Open** 10pm-3am daily. **Map** p99 F3 ⑦①

While the venue might not be as precious as the rare metal it's named after, it can still be tough to get into thanks to a stiff door policy. The music varies from Arabic to commercial R&B, the crowd can be hit and miss, but to check out the gold-plated dancefloor. It has to be seen.

I2

Metropolitan Hotel (04 343 0000, www. metropolitandubai.habtoorhotels.com). **Open** 8pm-3am daily. **Map** p98 B4 ⑦②

With a playlist that has both feet firmly in the '80s and '90s, an Alice in Wonderland interior and a fun but older fanbase, basement bar/club I2 is unlike any venue in Dubai.

Okku

The Monarch (04 501 8888, www. themonarchdubai.com) **Open** 7pm-3am daily. **Map** p99 F3 ⑦③

See p108 Eating & drinking.

Sensation

Crowne Plaza Dubai (04 331 1111, www.ichotelsgroup.com). **Open** 10pm-3am daily. **Map** p99 E4 ⑦④

Despite undergoing more name changes than P Diddy, Sensation has maintained a largely Lebanese crowd thanks to its soundsystem, impressive visuals and long-standing tech-house night, Neo, every Thursday.

Sublime

Ibis Hotel (04 318 7130, www. sublimebar.com). **Open** 6pm-3am daily. **Map** p99 E4 ⑦⑤

Despite opening as a South American themed meat restaurant Sublime has found more success hosting reggae and hip hop nights, while it also doubles up as the after-party of choice for events at the nearby Trade Centre.

Zinc

Crowne Plaza Dubai (04 331 1111, www.ichotelsgroup.com). **Open** 10pm-3am daily. **Map** p99 E4 ⑦⑥

Zinc's formula is simple - commercial music combined with cheap, or free, entry and a great location in the midst of Dubai. Wednesdays' ladies' night are the jewel in the crown thanks to the outstanding drink deals: a group of five or more ladies receive a free bottle of vodka, and there's free flowing champagne until 1am. Men have to pay full price for their drinks.

DUBAI BY AREA

Arts & leisure

Ayyam Gallery

Al Quoz (04 323 6242, www. ayyamgallery.com). **Open** 10am-8pm Sat-Thur. **Map** p98 A5 ⑰

A Syrian gallery offers contemporary art, with its country as the focus.

Carbon 12

Al Serkal Avenue, Al Quoz (050 464 4392, www.carbon12dubai.com). **Open** 11.30am-7pm Sat-Thur. **Map** p98 A5 ⑱

Shows modern artists with a European focus. Exhibitions tend to change fairly regularly which keeps things fresh here.

Cuadro

Gate Village 10, DIFC (04 425 0400, www.cuadroart.com). **Open** 10am-8pm Sun-Thur; noon-6pm Sat. **Map** p99 E4 ⑲

This huge space focuses on international art of all disciplines.

Dream Explorer

(04 331 9880, wwwdreamexplorerdubai. com). **Map** p99 F4 ⑳

High-powered jet boat tours to some of the main sights of Dubai, with a few high-speed, adrenaline-charged manoeuvres thrown in. Dhs185 per adult, Dhs140 per child.

Emirates Golf Club

Emirates Hills, Sheikh Zayed Road, (04 380 2222, www.dubaigolf.com). **Open** Majlis course 6am-3pm, Faldo course 6.15am-6pm daily. **Map** p98 A4 ㉛

The Emirates Golf Club boats two courses. The Majlis, the first grass course in the Middle East, is one of the top 100 golf courses in the world. The Faldo has full floodlighting. There's also a spa on site for a spot of post-fairway pampering.

Gallery Isabelle Van Den Eynde

Al Serkal Avenue, Al Quoz, (04 323 5052, www.ivde.net). **Open** 11am-7pm Sat-Thur. **Map** p98 A5 ㉜

The gallery (formerly B21) has gathered a wide portfolio, including some of Iran's most prominent artists.

Lawrie Shabibi Gallery

Al Serkal Avenue, Al Quoz, (04 346 9906, www.lawrieshabibi.com). **Open** 10am-6pm Sun-Thur. **Map** p98 A5 ㉝

New gallery that opened recently in Al Quoz, co-founded by one of the directors of the hugely successful Art Dubai annual festival, it showcases Middle Eastern works.

Safa Park

Between Sheikh Zayed and Al Wasl Roads, Jumeirah 2 (04 349 2111). **Open** 8am-11pm daily. **Admission** Dhs3. **Map** p98 B3 ㉞

The parks's circled by a 3.5km decent running track, where Dubai's professional footballers, abaya-clad power walkers and corporate joggers brush shoulders every night. Yet inside there's a lake with paddle boats, a rock garden, a maze (which is pretty easy to figure out) and plenty of swings, slides and barbecue areas. Perfect for a lazy winter afternoon.

Ayyam Gallery

Summertime Marine Sports

(04 257 3084, www.summertimemarine. com). **Map** p98 A4 ❽❺

The good people at Summertime handily provide pick-up and drop-off services. There's a minimum rental time of four hours and the cost includes bait, fishing equipment and crew. Summertime has two boats – one can carry up to 25 people, the other up to 30. Dhs2,000 for four hours boat hire.

thejamjar

Behind Dubai Garden Centre, Sheikh Zayed Road, Al Quoz (04 341 7303, www.thejamjardubai.com). **Open** 10am-8pm Sat-Thur; 2pm-8pm Fri. **Map** p98 A5 ❽❻

Contemporary art from local talent. Also offers regular DIY pick-up-and-paint sessions and community initiatives. A real thriving hub within the local arts scene.

The Spa at Fairmont Dubai

Fairmont Dubai, Sheikh Zayed Road, (04 311 8800, www.fairmont.com). **Open** 6am-midnight daily. **Map** p99 F3 ❻❼

Having had a recent revamp, expect high-quality pampering in Roman-themed surroundings. Facials cost from Dhs390.

The Spa at Shangri-La Dubai

Shangri-La Hotel, Sheikh Zayed Road (04 405 2441, www.shangri-la.com). **Open** 10am-10pm daily. **Map** p99 D3 ❻❽

Therapies are inspired by Asian healing philosophies. Separate facilities for men and women. Luxury facials start from around Dhs350 or treat yourself to a full day ritual and lunch deal.

The Third Line

Near The Courtyard, between Marlin Furniture and Spinney's, Al Quoz (04 341 1367, www.thethirdline.com). **Open** 10am-7pm Sat-Thur. **Map** p98 A5 ❻❾

Shows contemporary Middle Eastern art – one of the best galleries of its kind in the region. The Third Line represents around two dozen artists and also features the Projects exhibition space, which showcases local and Emirati artists.

Traffic

179 Umm Suqeim Road, Al Quoz, (04 347 0209www.viatraffic.org). **Open** 10am-8pm Sat-Thur. **Map** p98 A4 ❾⓪

The city's premium gallery for contemporary art, Traffic has built a solid reputation for the most cutting edge art in town. They also host annual showcases of local graduates of art and design courses.

Za'abeel Park

Sheikh Zayed Road (04 398 6888). **Open** 8am-11pm Sun-Wed; 8am-11.30pm Thur-Sat. **Admission** Dhs5. **Map** p99 F4 ❾❶

It cost nearly Dhs200 million to build and has a little something for everyone. For the more physically inclined among us, there are sizeable floodlit grass playing fields where sports teams can practice, as well as a cricket pitch to slog on. Meanwhile, recreational joggers can exercise on the 3.6km track, and there's also a skate park (of sorts) and BMX track as Za'abeel features a sizeable amphitheatre, which can be hired out for private events. For kids, there are numerous playgrounds featuring slides and jungle gyms, as well as pedal buggies for hire. Towards the south of the park, there's a large boating lake where you can hop onto a rowing or pedal boat and take to. And the fun doesn't stop there. Za'abeel is home to Stargate, the massive edutainment centre spread over five space themed domes, each packed with vaguely educational activities. There's also a couple of rollercoasters for kids with a sense of adventure.

DUBAI BY AREA

Jumeirah Mosque p115

Jumeirah & Satwa

Taking up the large expanse between Sheikh Zayed Road and the beach, Satwa and then Jumeirah are primarily residential areas. Most shops, cafés and restaurants are confined to Jumeirah Beach Road, which is a much more scenic and pleasant way to traverse the length of the city – if you have the time, thanks to some quite severe speed restrictions and rather a lot of traffic lights. This area is fantastic for getting a sense of the city away from the glittering high-rises and tourist attractions.

In the winter months lunch at a pavement café, followed by an afternoon on the beach is a favourite pastime of many residents. Thanks to the lack of huge developments (there are many malls, of course, but smaller ones) the area has fostered a smattering of independent boutiques, often homed in traditional villas, reworked to make shops. The Zoo and Bambah (opposite Dubai Zoo, see p118) are a small iceberg tip of a younger generation in the city who want a more personal, unique way to shop and who are after more than mass-produced items. Local designers often set up shop around here, as it's cheaper than trying to negotiate a space in a mall. Satwa remains a slightly rough around the edges, but much-loved, area of town. Home to Diyafah Road, a truly multicultural taste of the Middle East with its mix of cheap eats, electronic stores, tailors and – randomly – plant shops. Ravi's restaurant (see p123) on this street is a must for visitors – budget Pakistani food that's full of flavour and best enjoyed sat on the street, watching the world go by.

Jumeirah

Sights & museums

Dubai Zoo

Jumeirah Beach Road, Jumeirah 1 (04 349 6444). **Open** 10am-6pm daily, except Tue. **Admission** Dhs2. **Map** p116 C4 ❶

Dubai Zoo is very much 'old Dubai' – literally, as it hasn't changed in years, and even the entrance fee is an inflation-resistant Dhs2. Its fairly small site on Jumeirah Beach Road is home to around two dozen different exhibits, including big cats, giraffes, the obligatory reptile house, and an aviary. The aviary is probably the zoo's best feature, and has some exotic and attractive birds; otherwise the animals' conditions are cramped, to say the least. There are plans to move the zoo to a larger site, but these currently appear to be on hold. If you've got the time, head a little out town to Al Maha, where you'll find the Dubai Desert Conservation Reserve (www.ddcr.org, 04 832 9900).

Jumeirah Mosque

Jumeirah Beach Road, Jumeirah 1. **Open** 10am-11.30am Sat, Sun, Tue and Thur. **Map** p117 E3 ❷

Located at the northern end of Jumeirah Beach Road, it is arguably the most beautiful mosque in Dubai and has become a popular attraction. Tours of the mosque are organised by the Sheikh Mohammed Centre for Cultural Understanding (04 353 6666, www.cultures.ae) with an aim to promote cultural understanding and offer an insight into Islam. No prior booking is required – just show up on time and make sure you wear modest clothing (no bare arms or legs, and women must cover their heads).

Majlis Ghorfat Um Al Sheif

Jumeirah Beach Road, Jumeirah 3; look for nearby brown heritage signposts (04 394 6343). **Open** 8.30am-1.30pm, 3.30pm-8.30pm Sat-Thur; 3.30pm-8.30pm Fri. **Admission** Dhs1. **Map** p116 A4 ❸

Built in traditional style from coral and stone back in the 1950s, this two-storey building was used by the late Sheikh Rashid bin Saeed Al Maktoum as a home away from home. The house is furnished simply and offers a glimpse into what a life of luxury meant back then; the gardens are especially beautiful and you can see an example of the falaj – a traditional Arab irrigation system.

Eating & drinking

Ali Baba

Regent Beach Resort (04 344 5777). **Open** noon-midnight daily. $. **Middle Eastern. Map** p117 D3 ❹

Ali Baba is as surreal as it looks from the outside. The expansive interior is like a dinner hall, with row upon row of tables leading up to a small bar at the far end. Tinsel hangs from the ceiling, while flatscreen TVs line the walls, showing everything from the Action Channel to Lebanese soap operas.

Bu Qtair

Jumeirah Beach, Umm Suqeim. **Open** daily when catch arrives. $. **Seafood. Map** p116 A4 ❺

Hidden away behind Jumeirah Beach, in the corner of Dubai's fishermen's village, Bu Qtair looks more like an abandoned nursery. The only hint that this tiny shack could be a restaurant is a few multi-coloured kids' stools littered around the low plastic table. Bu Qtair doesn't have a phone number for calling ahead to book, or even a toilet, but it does serve some of the freshest fish in the Middle East – so fresh, in fact, that the menu changes every day, depending on the catch. If you don't mind taking a chance and come prepared for basic eating, it's worth a look.

Duck King p118

S*uce p119

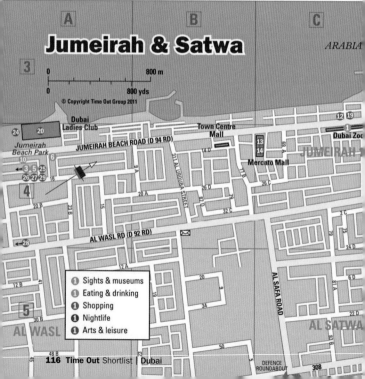

Jumeirah & Satwa

A **B** **C**

ARABIA

3

0 — 800 m

0 — 800 yds

© Copyright Time Out Group 2011

Dubai Ladies Club

Town Centre Mall

12 19

Dubai Zoo

24 20

Jumeirah Beach Park

JUMEIRAH BEACH ROAD (D 94 RD)

13
14

JUMEIRAH

6

Mercato Mall

3 5 25
26 27 29

4

AL WASL RD (D 92 RD)

26

AL SAFA ROAD

- ❶ Sights & museums
- ❶ Eating & drinking
- ❶ Shopping
- ❶ Nightlife
- ❶ Arts & leisure

AL WASL

AL SATWA

5

DEFENCE ROUNDABOUT

308

Satwa Park p124

Duck King

Beach Park Plaza Centre (04 342 8041).
Open 11am-11.30pm Sat-Wed;
11am-12.30am Thur-Fri. $$. **Asian.**
Map p116 A4 **6**

Go to Duck King for one thing – duck.
Order half a Peking duck and you're
first served the crispy skin with
fresh, thin pancakes and trimmings
(cucumber, hoi sin sauce, etc.). After
this, you can choose how the rest
of your duck is cooked. Opt for the
golden duck buns – sweet, ultra-rich
rolls stuffed with duck in a lovely
sticky marinade.

The Lime Tree Café

*Near to Jumeirah mosque, Jumeirah
1 (04 349 8498).* **Open** 7.30am-6pm
daily. $$. **Café.** **Map** p117 E3 **7**

Lime Tree's breakfasts, healthy
salads, huge puddings and cheesecake
are legendary. Now a chain with
various venues, this villa-based
original is still the best. In winter a
spot in the courtyard is a great way to
while away a weekend morning.

Long's Bar

*Towers Rotana, Sheikh Zayed Road
(04 312 2202).* **Open** noon-3am. $.
Pub. **Map** p117 D5 **8**

Home to the longest bar in the Middle
East, this is a rough 'n' ready pub,
popular with long time expats for
its cheap drinks deals. It also serves
decent enough pub grub and has a DJ
playing cheesy classics.

Saladicious

*Al Maskan building, Jumeirah (800
72523).* **Open** 8am-midnight daily. $.
Café. **Map** p117 E3 **9**

Relaxing boudoir chic with vintage
style frames, Vespa helmet ornaments,
and swirly patterned chairs adorn this
interesting little place, whilst chilled
music soothes your Dubai cares away.

Shu

Jumeirah Beach Road (04 349 1303).
Open 10am-2am Sat-Thur; 10am-3am
Fri. $$. **International.** **Map** p116
A4 **10**

Shu is all about the interior design:
even from the hip beige and brown
building it's obvious the inside is
going to be something extraordinary.
Bookcases line the walls, funky-
shaped furniture abounds and the
music is continually cool. And the
food? The menu is worryingly eclectic,
spanning everything from Italian to
Arabic, via sushi and Thai.

Shopping

Ayesha Depala

*The Village Mall, Jumeirah Beach
Road (04 344 5378).* **Open** 10am-
10pm Sat-Thur; 4.30pm-10pm Fri.
Map p117 D3 **11**

This Indian, Dubai-based designer's
clothes are all about silk, chiffon and
tulle – her gorgeous, girly dresses are
truly wearable. Worth a look if you
want to go home with something no
one else will have.

Bambah

*Jumeirah Beach Road, opposite Dubai
Zoo (04 349 5585).* **Open** 10am-
10pm daily. **Map** p116 C3 **12**

A girly vintage spot packed with
clothes from the '30s right through to
the '80s. There's also a large amount
of furniture collected from Egypt –
which is, unfortunately, not for sale.

Bullets & Butterflies

Mercato Mall (04 342 2243). **Open**
10am-10pm Sun-Wed, 10am-midnight
Thur-Sat. **Map** p116 C4 **13**

Two Emirati sisters own this unisex
(although its mostly womenswear)
boutique which sells brands such as
Stolen Girlfriend's Club from New
Zealand and Emirati menswear
designer Naz Cannon.

The Green Ecostore

Mercato Mall (04 344 4161). **Open**
10am-10pm Sun-Wed, 10am-midnight
Thur-Sat. **Map** p116 C4 **14**

A small stall in the Italian themed Mercato Mall (which isn't worth going out of your way for, but is a convenient mid-beach stop) sells only eco-friendly products.

Makeup Etc
Palm Strip Mall, Jumeirah 1 (04 345 5747). **Open** 10am-10pm Sat-Thur, 1.30pm-10pm Fri. **Map** p117 E3 ⑮

This small cosmetics boutique sells a range of brands you can't get in the rest of the city. We love Smith's Rosebud Salve – a true cure-all. They have a good range of organic products as well.

O Concept
Beach Residents Building, Shop Number Two, Jumeirah 1 (04 345 5557). **Open** 10am-10pm daily. **Map** p117 E3 ⑯

A locally owned design store that features fashion from across the region, plus homewares. There's a cute café there (as well as fantastic cupcake store, Sweet Stuff next door),

and it's right by the Jumeirah Mosque, so a good post-mosque tour pit stop.

THE One
Jumeirah Beach Road, next to the mosque (04 345 6687). **Open** 9am-10pm daily. **Map** p117 E3 ⑰

This locally grown homestore is somewhat of an institution in Dubai. The goods range from kitsch to classic, wooden to plastic – so basically they have everything. Make sure to try the deli upstairs for a cooling lemon with mint drink and a salad.

S*uce
The Village Mall, Jumeirah Beach Road (04 339 9696). **Open** 10am-10pm Sat-Thur; 4.30pm-10pm Fri. **Map** p117 D3 ⑱

Champions of local designers, this quirky store is always colourful (not just in the colour blocking seasons) and features cult overseas labels as well as up-and-coming designers from the region. It's not cheap but a visit to S*uce Lite, its outlet store across the road, is certainly less expensive.

The Lime Tree Café p118

Bullets & Butterflies p119

The One&Only Spa p121

The Zoo

Jumeirah Beach Road, opposite Dubai Zoo (04 349 5585). **Open** 10am-10pm daily. **Map** p116 C3 ⑲

This quirky design and gift store is right next door to vintage store Bambah and is full of designer toys, T-shirts, jewellery and more. A great place to pick up gifts. The owner and local designers are always sure to be hanging out, and make for interesting people to chat to.

Arts & leisure

Al Asalla Spa

Dubai Ladies Club, Jumeirah, (04 344 9445, www.dubailadiesclub. com). **Open** 9am-10pm daily. **Map** p116 A4 ⑳

The Decléor facial is great for a complexion boost but we love the hammam treatment – get scrubbed down in this traditional Moroccan ritual – you'll feel like a new woman. Women only (obviously).

Al Wasl Park

57th Street, off Al Wasl Road (04 344 0860). **Open** 8am-11pm daily; Fri-Sat families only; Sun-Thur ladies and children. **Admission** free. **Map** p117 D4 ㉑

Not to be confused with Safa, its much larger neighbour, the relatively diminutive Al Wasl Park is open throughout the week to ladies and children (men are allowed in at weekends with families). Small it may be, but there's still room for a few kids' playground areas and lots of shaded spots in which to relax – though we'll be hitting the sunnier patches to top up our fading tan. There's also plenty of room for runners and the park is open late, so it's an ideal location for an after-work jog. Perfect if you can't face doing a full circuit of one of the city's bigger spots, or are keen to avoid running near the roads.

Dubai Marine Beach Resort & Spa

Jumeirah Beach Road (04 346 1111). **Open** 7am-7pm daily. **Map** p117 E3 ㉒

Small but attractive beach, lush gardens and two swimming pools make it an ideal leisure venue, while its proximity to the city gives it the edge for beach-loving business travellers. Daily guests only have access to the private beach and pools. Day pass Dhs175 (Sat-Thur), Dhs220 (Fri). A lunch buffet can also be added to the day cost on if you get peckish.

Elche Natural Beauty Retreat

Behind petrol station near Spinneys, Jumeirah (04 349 4942, www.elche.ae) **Open** 10am-8pm Sat-Thur. **Map** p117 D3 ㉓

This lovely but rather expensive villa uses the organic Elche range. Facials start from Dhs640 – worth it for a special treat. They also offer a range of weight loss therapies.

Jumeirah Beach Park

Jumeirah Beach Road. **Open** 8am-10.30pm daily; open til 11pm Thur-Fri. **Admission** Dhs3 **Map** p116 A4 ㉔

One of the most popular of the city's parks as it sits next to the sea and offers beach frontage with the shade of some palm trees. There's also plenty of room for barbequing and a little shop selling ice cream and snacks. Get there early, though, if you want a picnic table and barbeque area.

The One&Only Spa

The One&Only Royal Mirage, opposite Media City, Jumeirah (04 399 9999, www.royalmirage-ssl.oneandonlyresorts.com). **Open** 9.30am-9pm daily. **Map** p116 A4 ㉕

Based on the architecture of ancient Arabia, this luxury spa is located in a domed building with spiral stone staircases. Get scrubbed at the oriental hammam downstairs – it's a must-do experience. Facials from Dhs495.

Showcase Gallery

Jumeirah Beach Road (04 348 8797). **Open** 9am-8pm Sat-Thur. **Map** p116 A4 ㉖

A converted villa selling international and Middle Eastern art, antiques, tribal jewellery and frames.

Surf Dubai

Burj Al Arab open beach, Jumeirah, (050 504 3020, www.surfingdubai.com). **Open** 9am-5pm daily **Map** p116 A4 ㉗

Park life

Dubai has green spaces if you know where to look.

While verdant lawns and areas of dense flora are not exactly synonymous with Dubai, there are a number of pleasant enough parks in which to while away the hours around the city. Creek Park (yep, you guessed it, by the creek), which costs Dhs5 to enter, is more than just a patch of grass, with activities including bike rentals for Dhs30 an hour, a park train, an 18-hole mini golf course, and an edutainment centre called Children's City. Fishing is also encouraged, with a jetty from which you can cast off into the creek. The biggest pulls here though are the dolphinarium, which offers sessions for swimming with dolphins, and the cable car along a partial stretch of the Creek. Over in Jumeirah, Safa Park (entry Dhs3) remains one of the city's most popular green spots, with a running track, a small lake with both motor and paddle boats, a maze, rock garden with waterfall and plenty of playgrounds for kids. During cooler months, it's also the site of Dubai's only Flea Market, which has grown enormously in popularity. Mirdif's Mushrif park, Dubai's largest, costs Dhs10 to enter with your car, you'll find a miniature international village stuffed with houses, a mini train, camel rides, a petting zoo and two good-sized segregated swimming pools. It's the city's oldest park, so parts may appear a little run down, but when so much of the city is new, we think it adds to this park's charm.

Dubai's oldest surf school offers lessons every day. Very popular on a Friday as they offer free taster lessons, so you'll need to book.

Thai Privilege Spa
Al Wasl Road, Jumeirah, (04 348 9679, www.thaiprivilege spadubai.com). **Open** 10am-10pm daily. **Map** p116 A4 ㉘

This spa is staffed by Thai reflexologists. Their reflexology treatments are some of the best in Dubai, whilst their traditional Thai massage is out of this world. The relaxing villa is a world away from the busy roads outside. Facials from Dhs250-300.

Wild Wadi
Jumeirah, (04 348 4444, www. wildwadi.com). **Open** daily 11am-9pm. **Map** p117 A4 ㉙

The Wild Wadi waterpark offers bodyboarding on artificially created waves specially designed for surfing. This slightly crazy, old looking water-fest is actually most residents' favourite over the slick Atlantis-based Aquaventure because of the lower entrance price and the lack of queues. Get there early to make a day of it. They also have ladies-only evenings during the summer. Dhs195 for entrance.

Satwa

Eating & drinking

Aussie Legends
Rydges Plaza (04 398 2222). **Open** 6pm-3am daily. $. **Pub. Map** p117 F4 ㉚

Aussie bar which is a local legend for its raucous but competitive Monday night quizzes. Drinks deals, ladies' night (Tuesdays), cheap pub grub and live music at the weekend are all

Wild Wadi

good reasons to pay a visit if you're in the area and want some rough 'n' ready fun.

Cactus Cantina

Rydges Plaza (04 398 2274). **Open** noon-1am daily. $$. **Tex-Mex.** Map p117 F4 ③①

You want everything covered in cheese? You've come to the right place. All the usual cuisine staples are here in large portions. Good for big groups of people looking to stodge-up before a night on the town.

Coconut Grove

Rydges Plaza (04 398 3800). **Open** noon-3pm, 7pm-midnight daily. $$. **Indian.** Map p117 F4 ③②

Popular with diners looking for a decent, licensed curry house in the Satwa area, Coconut Grove boasts a huge range of dishes from around the Indian subcontinent, including a great range of seafood options. There are few places more deserving of your custom if you've got your heart set on good quality seagfood at extremely reasonable prices.

Loca

Dubai Marine Beach Resort (04 346 1111, www.dxbmarine.com/ loca) **Open** midday-2am daily. $. **Bar.** Map p117 E3 ③③

As home to award-winning food, regular live music and DJs playing funk, soul, disco and indie at the weekends, Loca is regularly packed. It's also blessed with one of the best beer selections in the Middle East, including Heineken pumps at several of the tables.

Malecon

Dubai Marine Beach Resort (04 346 1111, www.dxbmarine.com/ malecon) **Open** 6pm-2am daily. $. **Bar.** Map p117 E3 ③④

A little erratic Cuban-themed restaurant and bar that serves lethal mojitos. Which perhaps explains the

scrawl that litters the wall as guests are allowed to graffiti the venue.

Noodle Bowl

Al Diyafah Road (04 345 3381). **Open** 8am-midnight daily. $. **Asian.** Map p117 F4 ③⑤

This charming Pan-Asian eatery may look like a simple little diner, but appearances can be deceptive. An airy and bright interior with punchy citrus hues and a café vibe also extends outside, with tables spilling across the pavement, from where you can soak up the hustle and bustle of Satwa.

Ravi's

Satwa Road (04 331 5353). **Open** 5am-3am daily. $. **Pakistani.** Map p117 E4 ③⑥

Ravi's is the local secret that's advertised on Emirates Airways – the 'insider' tip that people who've never been to Dubai know. Having said that, it's worth a visit nonetheless for no-nonsense, filling Pakistani curry on plastic plates, with plastic glasses, for crazy cheap prices.

Spectrum on One

The Fairmont (04 311 8101). **Open** 6.30pm-1am daily. $$$. **International.** Map p117 E5 ③⑦

A high-end international restaurant which serves up the best from a number of cuisines. If you're interested in trying a Dubai brunch, come on a Friday at midday and sample the best seafood, Asian, European and Indian delights – the restaurant even has a swanky cheese and port room and an in-house cigar bar.

Shopping

Book World

Plant Street (04 349 1914). **Open** 9.30am-9.45pm Sat-Thur; 4.30pm-9.45pm Fri. Map p117 E4 ③⑧

A second-hand bookstore that is full of character and hides the occasional gem. Worth a rummage.

Dar Al Hikma

Al Diyafah Road (04 349 9953).
Open 7am-11pm Sat-Thur, 7am-
10pm, 2pm-11pm Fri. **Map** p117 F4 **39**
A mainly Arabic bookstore housing
one of Dubai's best magazine
collections – we've never seen so
many Italian fashion glossies! Despite
appearance it stocks a large range of
international publications you won't
find anywhere else.

Deepak's

*Opposite Emirates Bank
(04 344 3536).* **Open** 9am-1.30pm,
4.15pm to 10.30pm Sat-Thur;
4.15pm-10.30pm Fri. **Map** p117 E4 **40**
This textile store was founded in
1977, and now has many branches
around Dubai. However, the Satwa
store is close to our hearts – and to
many tailors. The range of silks is
particularly mouthwatering.

Ishwal

*Alleyway that is first right after
Deepak's (04 349 2434).* **Open** 9am-
1pm, 4pm-10pm Sat-Thur; 4pm-10pm
Fri. **Map** p117 E4 **41**
There's just about room to swing a
couple of sewing machines (carefully)
in this tailors, a makeshift changing
room, some mammoth design
catalogues and lots and lots of clothes,
all peeping out of random carrier
bags. But there's a reason Deepak's
fabric store, and probably quite
a few of your well-dressed mates,
recommend Ishwal.

Plant Street

Map p117 E4 **42**
This nifty street near the Iranian
Hospital does what it says on the
tin – here you'll find a range of plant
shops. Even if you're not planning on
buying any plants, there are framers,
art shops and bagfuls of character on
offer. Take a wander and then plump
for one of the Pakistani restaurants
that surround the area for some much
cheap but tasty curry.

Nightlife

Boudoir

*Dubai Marine Beach Resort
(04 345 5995, www.myboudoir.com)*
Open 9pm-3am daily. **Map** p117
E3 **43**
A mainstay on the Dubai party circuit
thanks to a winning combination
of free champagne (for the ladies,
naturally), commercial – and very
cheesy – party tunes and a glitzy,
mock-French interior.

Sho Cho

*Dubai Marine Beach Resort
(04 346 1111, www.sho-cho.com)*
Open 6pm-3am daily. **Map** p117
E3 **44**
Ultra-slick sushi bar-cum-open air
club, Sho Cho is a popular hangout
with the rich and good looking in
Dubai. But don't let that put you off,
as the seaside perch is stunning and
the food and drinks excellent, if a little
over-priced.

Arts & leisure

Marsam Mattar

*Villa 21, 4B Street, Al Hudaibah
322, Satwa (04 398 8331, www.
marsammattar.com)*. **Open** 9am-
8.30pm Sat-Thur. **Map** p117 F4 **45**
Locally owned gallery focussing
on emerging Emirati talent and
covering mediums from oils and
watercolours through to video
installations and sculpture.

Satwa Park

308th Street (050 420 2892).
Open 8am-11pm Sat-Wed; 8am-
11.30pm Thur-Fri. **Map** p117 D5 **46**
While this green space may seem tiny
when you look at it from the outside,
once you step inside its boundaries
you'll find a sparkly new(ish) play
area, a full-size grass football pitch
(with nets), a running surface inside
the perimeter and, best of all, a
basketball and tennis court.

The world's oldest sport

Polo has found a natural home among riders in the UAE.

The sport of kings is often thought of as a quintessentially English pastime but it actually began over two thousand years ago, played both in Persia in the 5th century as a way to train cavalry, and in China. However, given the UAE's passion for all things equine it isn't a surprise that polo has taken off in a huge way in the last few years – with the sport finding its feet by attracting plenty of luxury sponsors. The polo season in Dubai runs between February and April, with some matches also being held in October and November and most events being held either at the Dubai Polo and Equestrian Club at Arabian Ranches (04 361 8111) or the Desert Palm hotel (04 323 8888), a boutique hotel with polo fields.

Dubai's eminent families often field teams, or they're made up of international players, depending on the level of the match. Lessons can be had at both the Desert Palm and the Dubai Polo and Equestrian Club, with the latter also offering a local twist on the sport – camel polo.

For many residents the polo matches are a good excuse to pack a picnic and spend the day stretched on a green field (a rarity in Dubai), catching up with friends over a bottle of wine and some food. Matches are held several times a week, including on Fridays and Saturdays and admittance is free. If you don't fancy slumming it on the field, you can book a table at the terraced restaurant and watch the chukkas in comfort. Once a year, the final match is held, usually in March or April, and the normally sedate club turns into a mini festival, complete with drinks lounges and an al fresco nightclub, whilst expats bring barbeques, gazebos and more to 'make a day of it'.

360

Al Barsha & Umm Suqeim

While Umm Suqeim is an older residential area of Dubai, populated by sprawling villas and residents lucky enough to have had plenty of Dubai boom years behind them, its neighbour across Sheikh Zayed Road, Al Barsha, has really started to come into its own in the last few years. Once the fairly desolate surroundings of the Mall of the Emirates, home to Ski Dubai (see p136), the area is now full of cheap apartment blocks. However, a handful of budget hotel chains (Ibis, Holiday Inn), independent restaurants, bakeries and shops are all slowly starting to open their doors – creating more of a community feel than that of a dusty sandpit. While views might

be thin on the ground in Barsha, it is centrally located for getting on the Metro and is halfway between Downtown and Dubai Marina – making most tourist attractions easily accessible. Back in Umm Suqeim, while not a shopping or cultural destination, it is home to the iconic Burj Al Arab (see p172), its neighbouring Jumeirah Beach Hotel, infamous club-out-at-sea, 360 (see p172) and soon luxury nightclub Mahiki's first venture outside of London. For kids and the young at heart, Dubai's oldest and much-loved waterpark Wild Wadi (see p172) is also located here. Down the coast you'll find surfers and kiteboarders using the consistent swell and winds off Sunset Beach.

Al Barsha

Eating & drinking

Après
Mall of the Emirates (04 341 2575).
Open 10am-1am daily. **$$**. **Bar**.
Map p128 B4 ❶
Where else but in Dubai could you order a hot chocolate, beer or pizza whilst overlooking an indoor ski slope or huddle round a fake fire, when it's hot, hot, hot outside? A haven in the summer months, Après' a cool hangout all year round.

Brick Lane
Al Barsha (04 399 6786).
Open 4pm-midnight daily. **$$**. **Indian**.
Map p128 A3 ❷
This British-style Indian curry house serves up lashings of thick, creamy tikka masala with greasy naan bread, just like you'd find back home. If you're a little homesick, this should help sort it out for you.

Gharana
Holiday Inn (04 323 4333). **Open** 7pm-11.30pm daily. **$$**. **Indian**. **Map** p128 B3 ❸
For a more authentic Indian meal try this hidden away number in

the Holiday Inn, which despite preconceptions about the brand, actually fields some decent restaurants. The menu's organised around regions of India but be warned – most dishes have more than a healthy bite to them.

Maxx Music Bar & Grill
Citymax hotel (04 409 8000). **Open** 11am-2am daily. **$**. **Pub**. **Map** p128 B4 ❹
Popular with both expats and holidaymakers, this budget hotel offers live music, sport on TV, karaoke, a pub quiz and drink deals – it'll be like you never left home.

Red Tomato Pizza
Near to Citymax hotel (800 866 286).
Open 11am-midnight Sun-Wed; 11am-1am Thur-Sat. **$**. **Italian**.
Map p128 B4 ❺
A kitsch independent Italian that offers, some would argue, the best pizzas in town from their wood-fired oven. And there's a delivery service.

The Royal Buddha
Holiday Inn (04 323 4333). **Open** 7pm-11.30pm daily. **$$**. **South East Asian**. **Map** p128 B3 ❻
This reasonably priced Thai is a little gem in Barsha as the restaurant fields

DUBAI BY AREA

Red Tomato Pizza

Al Barsha & Umm Sequim

Burj Al Arab **H**

40

Pte
Be

Mina A'Salam **H**
26

Palaces

Al Qasr **H**
25 30 31

Wild
Wadi

Jumeirah
Beach Hotel
34 **H**

Madinat
Jumeirah
27 28 29 32 33
35 41 42 43

AL SUFOUH ROAD
2

UMM
SUQEIM 3

UMM
AL SHEIF

UMM SUQEIM ROAD

Dubai Police
Academy

Interchange 4
(Exit 39)

3
H 17
19

(M)

H

Al Barsha
18

2

H 6 3

22

M

Mall of the
Emirates

Burj Al Arab **M**

Gold & Diamond
Park

H

Ski Dubai

H
1 7 8 9 10 11
12 13 14 20 23 24

Mall of the
Emirates

8

AL BARSHA

4
16

15

4
5

H

H

H

H

H

Al Barsha
Park

UMM SUQEIM ROAD

38

❶	Sights & museums
❶	Eating & drinking
❶	Shopping
❶	Nightlife
❶	Arts & leisure

5

WHEN THE SUN GOES DOWN

THE STARS
COME OUT
TO PLAY

LOUNGE | DRINKS | DJ

AT.MOSPHERE
THE LOUNGE

Live DJ, sensational drinks and spectacular views
at The Lounge. Join the in crowd at At.mosphere,
Dubai's highest social hotspot. Open 12pm to 2am,
no reservations required.

THIS IS WHERE IT'S AT.

AT.MOSPHERE
T +971 4 888 3828
E reservations@atmosphereburjkhalifa.com

Tribes

an above average array of South Asian delights, with a focus on fish.

Sanabel
Pullman Hotel, Mall of the Emirates (04 377 2000). **Open** 12pm-4pm; 6.30pm-11pm daily. **$$.** **International.** Map p128 B4 ❼
Large international dining restaurant with a focus on more healthy dishes. Every ingredient appears well sourced, well picked and fresh and there's a real sense of genuine appreciation for good food from the kitchen through to the waiters.

St Maxim's
Mall of the Emirates (04 341 3415). **Open** noon-1am daily. **$$.** **Steakhouse.** Map p128 B4 ❽
Although it's in a mall St Maxim's has its fans locally thanks to a decent array of steaks on offer, which won't break the bank, unlike most other steakhouses in the city.

Tribes
Mall of the Emirates (04 395 0663). **Open** 11.30am-12.30pm daily. **$$.** **South African.** Map p128 B4 ❾

Tribes brings a touch of South African flavour to the Mall of the Emirates' offerings. A chain, its décor is distinctive savannah chic, complete with faux-fur throws over chairs and rustic pottery-style plates, but there's nothing too scary about this place, apart from the waiters' occasionally random drumming and singing. A haven for meat lovers.

Shopping

Ai Zone
Mall of the Emirates, Barsha (04 347 9333). **Open** 10am-10pm Sun-Wed; 10am-midnight Thur-Sat. Map p128 B4 ❿
This huge unisex fashion store has its own travelator, but we also like it for its quirky brands – from international brands like Melissa+Campana and American Retro to more regional labels.

Boom & Mellow
Mall of the Emirates, Barsha (04 341 3993). **Open** 10am-10pm Sun-Wed, 10am-midnight Thur-Sat. Map p128 B4 ⓫

DUBAI BY AREA

This cute in-mall jewellery boutique sells the best of regional and international designers. We love it because it's such a unique find for the middle of Mall of the Emirates.

Carrefour
Mall of the Emirates, Barsha
(04 409 4899). **Open** 10am-10pm
Sun-Wed, 10am-midnight Thur-Sat.
Map p128 B4 ⑫
This giant hypermarket is loved and loathed by residents. If you're looking for cheap electronics, Carrefour should be your first port of call. Often heavily discounted laptops, mobiles and cameras all come with a one year guarantee.

Fashion Dome
Mall of the Emirates, Barsha
(04 409 9000). **Open** 10am-10pm
Sun-Wed, 10am-midnight Thur-Sat.
Map p128 B4 ⑬
A new extension to this older (in Dubai terms) mall, Fashion Dome features boutiques for Christian Louboutin,

Michael Kors, DVF and more. It's a must-visit for anyone with a sartorial bent.

Harvey Nichols
Mall of the Emirates, Barsha
(04 409 8888). **Open** 10am-10pm
Sun-Wed, 10am-midnight Thur-Sat.
Map p128 B4 ⑭
The classic Dubai boutique, this three storey store is always worth a visit. Be sure not to miss its gorgeous Moroccan restaurant, Almaz by Momo, which is a hot spot for sheesha and people-watching amongst the local crowd.

Pinky Furniture
Opposite Dubai American Academy
(04 422 1720). **Open** 10am-8pm
Sun-Mon, Wed-Thur; 2pm-8pm Fri.
Map p128 B4 ⑮
This independent Indian import store features a range of wooden furniture – some painted with Ganesh or Indian Goddesses – that is affordable and of good quality.

Fashion Dome

Skydiving in Dubai

Experience the thrill of freefall from a plane. Or in a mall.

It might not be the first thing you'd expect a royal heir to be enthused about, but Dubai's only – and relatively new – outdoor skydiving centre, Skydive Dubai, is owned by none other than Crown Prince of Dubai His Highness Sheikh Hamdan bin Mohammed bin Rashid Al Maktoum, who is a keen and accomplished participant in the sport.

Located in Dubai Marina, the centre runs two small aircraft to take both skilled and amateur divers to a height of around 13,000ft. If you're not qualified, you'll jump as a tandem, strapped to the front of a professional diver who will nonchalantly dangle you out of the door before launching you both out. If you're going to dive anywhere in the world, it's worth a go in Dubai for the view.

During your one minute freefall and subsequent descent under a parachute, you'll get an incredible bird's eye view of the Palm Jumeirah. But if 13,000ft feels a little too high (we won't hold it against you), and you're willing to sacrifice the aesthetic elements of the experience, Mirdif City Centre's indoor skydiving centre is a less daunting way of getting your buzz. The iFly wind tunnel offers that freefall feeling for a fraction of the cost, and a much longer freefall feeling – and of course none of the danger as you're only a metre or two from the ground in a controlled air tunnel.

■ Skydive Dubai, Dubai Marina (050 153 3222, www.skydivedubai.com), Dhs1,700 per person, including DVD and digital still pictures.

■ iFly Dubai, Mirdif City Centre, Mirdif (04 231 6292, www.iflyme.com) Dhs195 per person for first time flyers.

Ductac p135

There aren't many small trinkets, however, so only head here if you're staying in Dubai for a while.

Smiles 'N Stuff

Barsha (04 340 4844). **Open** 9am-2pm, 4pm-7pm Wed-Mon. **Map** p128 B4 ⑯

This store sells the handicrafts of Al Noor Training Centre for Children with Special Needs, whose students also work in the shop.

Nightlife

Casa Latina

Ibis Al Barsha (04 399 6699). **Open** 6pm-2.30am daily. **Map** p128 A3 ⑰

Once a backwater bar, Casa Latina is now a thriving alternative hub with Freshly Laced playing funk, soul and hip-hop every Thursday and Loaded bringing a monthly indie edge every last Friday of the month.

Catwalk

Golden Tulip Al Barsha (04 341 7750). **Open** 8pm-3am daily. **Map** p128 A3 ⑱

Underground clubs are few and far between in Dubai, which makes Catwalk all the more worthy. Wednesdays play host to dubstep and D n' B, while Thursdays host a variety of promoters who push various strands of tech-house.

Rock Bottom

Ramee Rose Hotel (04 450 0111, www.rameehotels.com). **Map** p128 A3 ⑲

See p88 Rock Bottom, Bur Dubai.

Arts & leisure

DUCTAC

Mall of the Emirates (04 341 4777, www.ductac.org). **Map** p128 B4 ⑳

A fantastic community arts centre and theatre showing dance, drama and comedy, plus classes in everything from African drumming to painting.

Breath and Health

Al Wasl Road, Umm Suqeim (04 348 9940). **Open** 10am-8pm daily. **Map** p129 E2 ㉑

A great villa spa that offers everything from Ayurvedic head massages to acupuncture and specialises in many different holistic therapies.

Marine Concept

Rania Business Centre, office 401, Barsha, (055 960 3030, www. marine-charter-concept.com). **Open** 9am-6pm daily. **Map** p128 B3 ㉒

A boat company with a varied fleet of boats that can be commissioned for fishing trips. Captain, crew, equipment, soft drinks and water included in the price. Dhs3,000 for a four-hour chartered fishing trip.

Sanctuary Spa

Pullman Dubai Mall of the Emirates, Barsha (04 377 2000). **Open** 10am-10pm daily. **Map** p128 B2 ㉓

A gorgeous new addition to Dubai's pampering scene, this Barsha-based spa has a gorgeous infinity pool. Facials from Dhs250. Check out one of the pool bars afterwards for a stunning view, right across to Umm Suqeim and the Burj Al Arab..

Ski Dubai

Mall of the Emirates, Barsha, (04 409 4333, www.skidxb.com). **Open** 10am-11pm Sun-Wed; 10am-midnight Thur; 9am-midnight Fri; 9am-11pm Sat. **Map** p128 B4 ㉔

The first ski resort in the Middle East, inside Mall of the Emirates, offers skiing, snowboarding, tobogganing and, of course, playing in the snow. You can even try Zorbing (whizzing downhill inside an inflatable ball).It costs Dhs180 for two hours; Dhs300 for an adult day pass. A must for any first time visitors, if only for the photo opportunities, to cool down and to have a yummy hot chocolate in the café halfway up the artificial slope.

Pierchic p136

Umm Suqeim

Eating & drinking

Al Hambra
Al Qasr Hotel (04 366 6730). **Open**
Mon-Sat 7pm-11.30pm. **$$**. **Spanish**.
Map p128 B2 ㉕
Reasonable and tasty tapas at this
high-end Spanish restaurant in the
opulent hotel. A small menu hides
some decent gems, plus food and
drinks deals are always on.

Bahri Bar
*Mina A'Salam, Madinat Jumeirah (04
366 6730).* **Open** 6pm-3am daily. **$$**.
Bar. **Map** p128 B2 ㉖
Though it could be described as one
of Madinat Jumeirah's least celebrated
bars, Bahri Bar is surely one of its best.
While you're tucking into delicious
snacks and creative sundowners,

a beautiful wrap-around terrace
provides perfect views of the Burj –
best seen during its chameleon-like
light show at night – and overlooks a
fine stretch of sea and sand.

Barzar
Souk Madinat Jumeirah (04 366 6197).
Open 4pm-3am Fri; 5pm-3am Tue &
Thu; Wed 5pm-2am Sat-Mon. **$**. **Bar**.
Map p128 B2 ㉗
An after-work favourite with Dubai's
younger crowd of office boys and
girls, this bar gets extremely busy on
Tuesdays and Thursdays thanks to a
plethora of drinks deals throughout
the week, good music and a large
waterside veranda scattered with
great big comfy beanbags.

Left Bank
Souk Madinat Jumeirah (04 368 6171).
Open noon-1.30am daily. **$**. **Bar**.
Map p128 B2 ㉘

Another waterside spot in Madinat Jumeirah, Left Bank is both restaurant and bar, with an excellent variety of dishes on the menu, each arriving in generous portions. While the bar has a tendency to get a little crowded on busier nights like Fridays, the drinks are reasonable enough and if you manage to nab a table next to the water outside, we'd wager you'll find little to complain about.

The Meat Co

Madinat Jumeirah (04 368 6040). **Open** 11am-11.30pm Sat-Wed; 1pm-12.30am Thur-Fri. **$$. Steakhouse.** Map p128 C2 ㉙

This restaurant means business when it comes to steak. It has become a Dubai institution – it even has a celebrity following, the names of whom can be found scrawled on plates adorning the walls of the Madinat venue (our favourite is Jordan's barely legible 'signature').

Pai Thai

Al Qasr Hotel (04 366 6730). **Open** 7pm-11.30pm daily. **$$$. Thai.** Map p128 B2 ㉚

First things first: make sure you take the abra option to get to this Thai restaurant – you'll impress not only your company, but yourself with the peaceful waters of the vast Madinat Jumeirah canals, and the twinkly lights of the resort. Then order some excellent Thai food and get stuck in.

Pierchic

Al Qasr Hotel (04 366 6730). **Open** 7pm-11.30pm daily. **$$$. Seafood.** Map p128 B2 ㉛

Literally a chic restaurant, at the end of a pier into the Gulf, Pierchic specialises in fish and romance. But be sure to request an outdoor table at the front of the restaurant; if you're seated towards the back, the tall wooden barriers surrounding the pier mean that you have to strain to peer through the windows.

Pisces

Madinat Jumeirah (04 366 8888). **Open** 7pm-11.30pm daily. **$$. Seafood.** Map p128 B2 ㉜

Even from its Madinat Jumeirah frontage, Pisces has a stylish air and inside doesn't disappoint either, with a seaside-blue colour scheme and soft music. There's also a scenic outdoor area, protected by palm trees. One of Dubai's superior fish eateries; Pisces is a place you'll certainly leave with a huge sailor's smile.

Segreto

Madinat Jumeirah (04 366 6730). **Open** 7pm-11.30pm daily. **$$$. Italian.** Map p128 C2 ㉝

From the romantic waterside setting (you arrive by abra) to understated but sumptuous décor, attentive (but not too fussy) waiters and first-rate cuisine, Segreto is hard to find fault with – which is what you would expect from *Time Out* Dubai's most romantic restaurant. Tasteful and tasty, the menu is inspiring in its simplicity.

Uptown Bar

Jumeirah Beach Hotel (04 406 8999). **Open** 7pm-2am daily. **$$. Bar.** Map p128 C2 ㉞

Positioned at the top of the wave-shaped Jumeirah Beach Hotel, Uptown may have awkward opening hours (if you're there any earlier than 7pm, you'll be left loitering in the corridors outside the executive lounge) but it's certainly worth hanging around for. Its outdoor terrace serves up delicious cocktails and surprisingly reasonable drinks, along with views down the coast and, on clear nights, right over to Business Bay.

The Wharf

Madinat Jumeirah (04 366 6730). **Open** 7pm-11.30pm daily; 12.30pm-4pm Fri. **$$. British.** Map p128 B2 ㉟

The Wharf's selling point is its outdoor seating area – think Brit beer garden with Arabic characteristics. The food sits firmly in the Brit gastropub zone – pies, Yorkshire puddings, foie gras and pork belly.

Shopping

If Boutique
26 Umm Al Sheif Street (04 394 7260). **Open** 10am-9pm Sat-Thur. **Map** p129 F2 ③⑥
A dramatic, concrete-floored high-end fashion store that features lines from a range of one-off and avant garde designers such as Comme Des Garçons, Tsumori Chusato, Anne Demeulemeester and Junya Watanabe.

Kartell
Villa 746, Jumeirah Beach Road (04 348 8169). **Open** 10am-8pm Sat-Thur. **Map** p129 E2 ③⑦
This high-end Italian furniture boutique sells classics like the Ghost chair, as well as the brand's more unusual rubber shoes. High design

sadly doesn't come cheap, however – everything is pricey in Kartell.

Marina Exotic Home Furniture
Umm Suqeim Road, Al Quoz (04 340 1112). Open 9am-8.30pm daily. **Map** p128 C5 ③⑧
A huge interiors warehouse with modern furniture as well as rustic pieces like giant Omani, Pakistani and Indian doors, which we just wish we had a house big enough for.

O'De Rose
Villa 999, Al Wasl Road (04 348 7990). **Open** 10am-8pm Sat-Thur. **Map** p129 D2 ③⑨
This Lebanese-owned boutique, hidden away on an Umm Suqeim street, is full of trinkets, clothes and furniture from across the Levantine and North Africa. If you have an eye for design from the region, this is the one store to visit. It's not cheap, but the pieces you buy from here are ones you'll cherish for a long time.

Segreto p137

Nightlife

360

Jumeirah Beach Hotel (04 406 8744, www.jumeirah.com). **Open** 4pm-2am daily. **Map** p128 C1 ⓸

Voted as one of the best clubs in the world on several occasions, 360 offers panoramic views of Dubai's etch-a-sketch skyline and the Burj, and has a soundtrack to match with house, funk and disco all on offer.

Jambase

Madinat Jumeirah (04 366 6914, www.jumeirah.com) **Open** 7pm-2am daily. **Map** p128 B2 ⓶

A refined supper club offering good food, but sometimes stretched service, especially when it's busy as it can be at the weekends. But with an excellent live band, and a smooth transition from dinner to dancefloor, few venues can compete.

Trilogy

Madinat Jumeirah (04 336 6917, www.trilogy.ae) **Open** 10pm-3am Mon-Sat. **Map** p128 B2 ⓸

Dubai's leading club returned after a two year hiatus, and has lost none of its charm. The Rooftop terrace is still stunning, the weekend bookings impressive (Mark Ronson re-opened the club) and the crowd are consistently up for it.

Arts & leisure

Madinat Theatre

Madinat Jumeirah (04 366 6546, www.madinattheatre.com). **Map** p128 C2 ⓸

Dubai's only large scale theatre can be found at the Madinat complex. It hosts travelling productions of large scale plays and musicals which, although busy, tend to only run for a few nights. Recent productions have included *Hairspray* and *Mamma Mia!* The venue also puts on local shows with amateur and kids' drama groups.

March on

If waterparks and malls aren't your bag, fear not.

If you're a culture vulture, there's only one time to come to Dubai – March. Over recent years more and more huge annual events have slid into this month, which usually guarantees perfect weather. From Taste of Dubai – a multi-day event where the city's finest restaurants set up shop to offer cheap taster meals alongside celebrity chef workshops and a gourmet marketplace, to the International Jazz Festival, which has brought Grays, both David and Macy, to Dubai in recent years, the month is jam-packed with unique things to do. In addition to that the annual Art Dubai show has now extended to bring together all the galleries in the city in an umbrella event called (confusingly) Art Week. Hop on an art bus which'll take you on a tour of the city, hit a film screening or check out lively discussions organised as part of the programme. And to top it all off, the Emirates Airline Festival of Literature also rolls into town, bringing with it globally renowned authors such as Michael Palin and Margaret Atwood.

Dubai Marina

Dubai Marina & The Palm

The centre of new Dubai, Dubai Marina is an incredible development considering there was nothing at all up this end of town apart from the now empty and forgotten Hard Rock Cafe (although a newer, updated version should be opening at Festival City soon). Along the beach runs The Walk, a strip designed for pedestrians and those that want to cruise in their Ferraris, full of reasonabley priced cafes and restaurants and a smattering of hotels. While the ground floor restaurants offer plenty of people watching, if you want a drink with your meal, head into one of the hotels. Behind The Walk sits Jumeirah Beach Residence (JBR). This sprawling complex of 30

odd skyscrapers, plaza levels and pools is home to a huge number of Western expats and it takes up the entire space between the beach and the marina. Behind the marina sits yet more residential skyscrapers, but the best place to appreciate the dazzling architecture is on Marina Walk, which runs the entire length of the marina. Joggers, cyclists and exercise classes frequently make use of this space, whilst those after more of a sedate evening head to the Dubai Marina Yacht Club's terrace to watch the million dollar yachts gently bob (see p141).

The Palm (or Palm Jumeirah) really needs no introduction. An extensive man-made island, it's only recently come into its own with more bars and restaurants opening along the right hand side. Although the recession has hit the villa fronted 'fronds' hard, with many villas now being empty or rented out for relatively rock bottom prices, the apartments have faired better and the main trunk of the Palm is consistently busy. New hotel openings the One&Only The Palm and Jumeirah Zabeel Saray (see p174) have cemented it as a destination again, joining the rather tacky Atlantis (see p174).

Dubai Marina

Eating & drinking

AOC French Brasserie
Sofitel Dubai Jumeirah Beach, Dubai Marina (04 448 4848). **Open** 6.30am-10.30am, 12.30pm-3.30pm, 7pm-11pm daily. **$$**. **French**. **Map** p142 B4 ❶
We love the 30 minute lunch – a four course meal sampler. Too quick? Think about Brunch à la Française with crêpes, croissants, baguette bread, signature dishes – all for only around Dhs200.

Aquara Lounge
Dubai Marina Yacht Club (04 362 7900). **Open** 6pm-midnight daily. **$$**. **Bar**. **Map** p142 A5 ❷
Few places with a daily happy hour see their premises as popular as this waterfront spot. Lively throughout the week – and frankly crazy on Thursday evenings – there's a very decent variety of wine on the menu, and when it's cool enough, the terrace looking out over the marina makes it a romantic spot.

Bar 44
Grosvenor House (04 399 8888). **Open** 6pm-2am Fri-Wed; 6pm-3am Thur. **$$**. **Bar**. **Map** p142 B5 ❸
One of the Marina's longest established bars, it's a less smoky

rival to the downstairs Buddha Bar, but equally worth visiting. Positioned on the 44th floor (the clue's in the name) of the Grosvenor House hotel, expect extraordinary views over the surrounding marina.

Barasti
Le Meridien Mina Seyahi Beach Resort & Marina (04 399 3333). **Open** 11am-2am daily. **$$**. **Bar**. **Map** p142 C4 ❹
Infamous local bar, Barasti, is the first place you should hit for a night out on the sand. Split between an upper level which includes an al fresco restaurant, sofas and a pool and a more clubbing inspired lower level, Barasti is the one place where Dubai's party people come together as one. The beach has recently seen the introduction of a permanent stage and acts from Vanilla Ice to The Streets have hit it.

Bussola
The Westin Mina Seyahi (04 399 4141). **Open** noon-2.45pm, 7pm-10.45pm daily. **$$**. **Italian**. **Map** p142 C4 ❺
If you're hankering for Italian food but can't choose between a casual, rustic pizza or a more upmarket, fine-dining affair, Bussola is your go-to spot. The venue, nestled amid the Westin's lush gardens and multiple pools, boasts an open-air terrace upstairs, offering panoramic views of Palm Jumeirah.

Frankie's
Al Fattan Towers, The Walk (04 399 4311). **Open** 12.30pm-4pm, 6pm-1.30am daily. **$$**. **Italian**. **Map** p142 B4 ❻
Frankie's – the byproduct of collaboration between Marco Pierre White and jockey Frankie Dettori – delivers on every front. The atmosphere is lively and vibrant and the food fitting of the restaurant's rich decadent decor.

Grand Grill
Habtoor Grand Resort & Spa (04 399 4221). **Open** 1pm-midnight daily. **$$$**. **Steakhouse**. **Map** p142 B4 ❼

Dubai Marina & The Palm

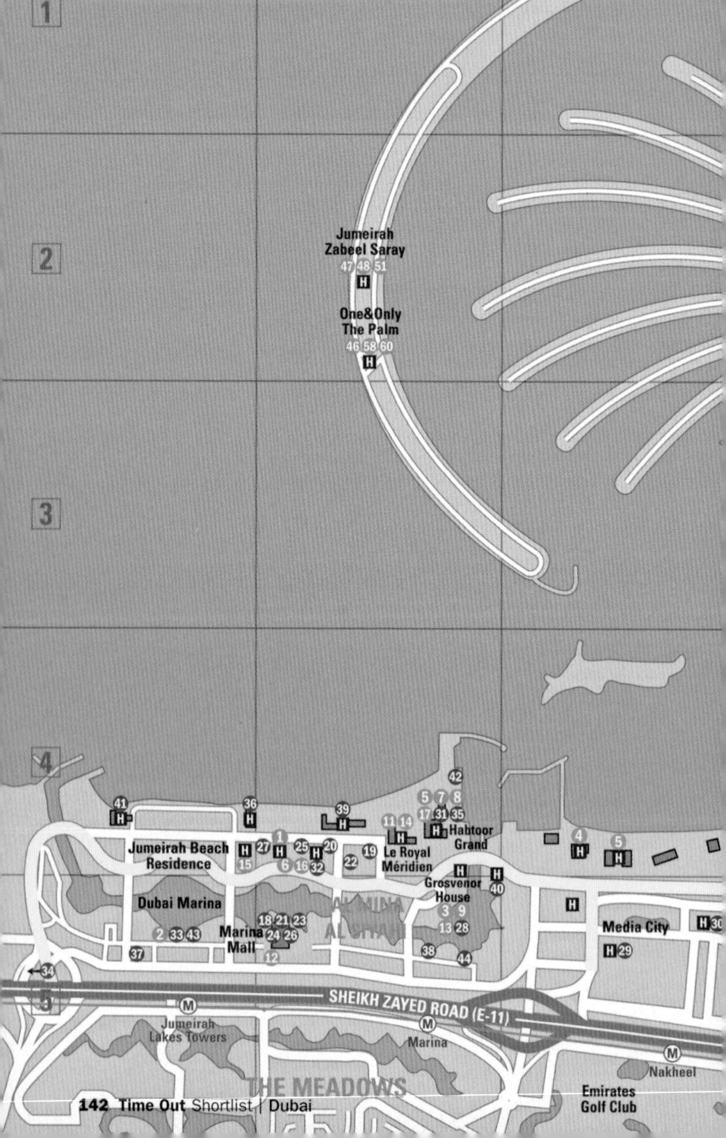

Jumeirah
Zabeel Saray
47 48 51
Ⓗ

One&Only
The Palm
46 58 60
Ⓗ

42

5 7
31
17 31 35
11 14   Habtoor
Grand

36

39

Jumeirah Beach
Residence
Ⓗ 27 1 25 20
15   16 32   19
Le Royal
Méridien

Grosvenor
House
9 3
13 28
Ⓗ

41
Ⓗ

Dubai Marina

18 21 23
2 33 43   24 26
Marina   12
Mall

40
Ⓗ

4
Ⓗ
5
Ⓗ

38   44

Media City
Ⓗ 29

30
Ⓗ

37
34

SHEIKH ZAYED ROAD (E-11)

Jumeirah
Lakes Towers

Marina

Nakheel

THE MEADOWS

Emirates
Golf Club

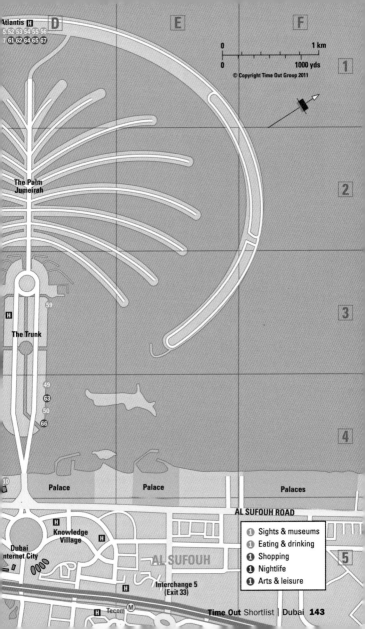

Rosso p145

Bussola p141

A combination of low lighting, dark woods and a scattering of tribal accessories (this steakhouse has a vaguely African theme) makes Grand Grill a warm and inviting venue. Since steak is the name of the game, order the 300g New York sirloin, it'll be pert, pink and juicy.

Horizon
Habtoor Grand Resort & Spa.
Open 10am-2am daily. **$$**. **Bar**. Map p142 B4 **8**
The party atmosphere at this al fresco bar prevails throughout the week, thanks to an enormously popular mid-week ladies' night (free champagne and strawberries for the fairer sex) and spirited performances from the DJs behind the decks on Thursdays. As an aside, it seems there's no such thing as overdressed in this bar, so be sure to leave your inner conservative (and prude) at home.

Indego by Vineet
Grosvenor House (04 399 8888).
Open 7.30pm-midnight daily. **$$$**.
Indian. Map p142 B5 **9**
Combine Michelin-starred chef Vineet Bhatia's fusion of traditional Indian and contemporary European cuisine with an über-sophisticated setting and you have a winning formula on your hands – which may explain why Indego is such a hit with Dubai's discerning crowds.

Jetty Lounge
One&Only Royal Mirage, Al Sufouh Road (04 399 9999) **Open** 2pm-1am daily. **$$**. **Bar**. Map p143 D4 **10**
This recently opened beach bar brings a much need touch of sophistication to the sand. Set apart from the hotel, arrive by hotel buggy and amidst the twinkling lights, find comfy white sofas, beanbags down on the sand, and a sleek looking bar, for when you can't find a waiter. Bar snacks sit at the high end, so think sushi and so on, whilst the cocktails are divine.

Maya by Richard Sandoval
Le Royal Meridien Beach Resort & Spa, Dubai Marina (04 399 5555). **Open** 7.30pm-midnight Mon-Sat. **$$$**.
Mexican. Map p142 B4 **11**
Elegant Maya, the crisp white interior being your first clue that this ain't no ordinary Mexican. It's sophistication over sombreros here. It is also one of the few places brave enough to serve mole pablano – chicken in chocolate

sauce, essentially – and the rendition of the dish is a delight, sneaking in just enough fire to balance the sweetness of swathes of sinfully dark cocoa.

Puerto del Elite

The Address Marina (04 436 7777).
Open 6pm-midnight Sun-Thur; 6pm-2am Fri-Sat. **$$**. **Bar**. **Map** p142 B5 ⑫
Far from the bean-bagged terrace we once knew as Shades, Puerto de Elite has gone all out in its bid to bring Mediterranean club style to the Middle East. Admittedly the prevalence of white in the open-air club-lounge-restaurant is a little overwhelming at first, but they've certainly headed in the right direction since opening at the beginning of December.

Rhodes Mezzanine

Grosvenor House (04 399 8888).
Open 7.30pm-11.30pm Mon-Sat. **$$$$**.
British. **Map** p142 B5 ⑬
The restaurant's dazzling, porcelain white décor gives a visual indication of the food served within – whch is nearly as flawless as the aesthetic, embellishing old-world culinary values with flashes of modernity.

Rhodes Twenty10

Le Royal Meridien Beach Resort & Spa (04 399 5555). **Open** 7pm-midnight Tue-Sun. **$$$$**. **Steakhouse**.
Map p142 B4 ⑭
There are three ingredients that practically guarantee a successful restaurant in Dubai: steak, a celebrity chef connection and ritzy decor. If a venue can claim one of these, chances are it's going to do all right. Beware the of blatant up-selling and an over-inflated bill here though.

Rosso

Amwaj Rotana (04 428 2000).
Open 6pm-1am daily. **$$**. **Italian/Bar**. **Map** p142 A4 ⑮
An Italian restaurant and bar, Rosso may seem from the outside like any other hotel pizzeria, but step outside onto the terrace it shares with neighbouring Japanese joint Benihana, and it's possible you'll forget you're in Dubai at all as you settle into a comfy chair on the (fake) grass. A great escape from the traffic chaos on The Walk beachfront promenade, the venue also runs daily happy hours and ladies' night deals.

Rhodes Mezzanine

DUBAI BY AREA

Desigual

Trader Vic's Mai Tai Lounge

Trader Vic's Mai Tai Lounge

Al Fattan Towers (04 399 8993).
Open 6pm-2.30am daily. $$. **Bar**.
Map p142 B4 ⑯

While it may boast a great selection of lethal mixed drinks, the live band who play frequently at this Polynesian-themed nightspot do a good job of drowning out conversations and making you wish you'd gone somewhere else instead.

The Underground

Habtoor Grand Resort & Spa (04 399 5000). **Open** noon-3am daily. $$. **Pub**. **Map** p142 B4 ⑰

A popular spot with football fans (it's a Liverpool pub), The Underground is relatively quiet most days of the week, but draws big crowds on match days, doing a roaring trade in pints, chips and bangers and mash. The pool tables are always a popular draw too.

Shopping

Billabong

Dubai Marina Mall (04 434 2577).
Open 10am-10pm daily. **Map** p142 B5 ⑱

The surf inspired Australian chain has a store here for last minute beachwear items, if you forgot your cossie.

Boutique 1

JBR The Walk (04 425 7888). **Open** 10am-11pm daily. **Map** p142 B4 ⑲

This gorgeous three level store sells super stylish brands and encompasses homewares, fashion, accessories and more. There's a spa and plenty to see, so give yourself some time (if you have money to burn).

Cottage Chic

JBR The Walk (04 438 0473). **Open** 10am-10pm Sun-Weds, Fri; 10am-midnight Thur, Sat. **Map** p142 B4 ⑳

This locally owned one-off store is perfect for anyone who loves floral material, floral sofas and cushions with, erm, flowers on them. It's shabby chic at its most cutesy chic.

Desigual

Dubai Marina Mall (04 399 7893).
Open 10am-10pm daily. **Map** p142 B5 ㉑

For quirky Spanish fashion which takes influences from the '70s and ethnic clothing look no further.

Indigo Living

Sadaf Plaza, JBR (04 428 1350).
Open 10am-10pm Sat-Thur; 3.30pm-10pm Fri. **Map** p142 B4 ㉒

This homewares store is originally from Hong Kong and sells a range of

Boutique 1 p146

quirky pop style Asian homewares – from neon coloured panda canvases to giant Buddha heads. The JBR branch is a true hidden gem as it often has great sales – last summer there was 75 per cent off everything.

Juicy Couture
Dubai Marina Mall (04 434 2638). **Open** 10am-10pm daily. **Map** p142 B5 ㉓
For the latest blinging velour tracksuits or Hollywood style handbags, hit Juicy Couture, the cult American label that's found a natural home in the Middle East.

Kurt Geiger
Dubai Marina Mall (04 399 7880). **Open** 10am-10pm daily. **Map** p142 B5 ㉔
For skyscraper heels without skyscraper prices, head to this chain of reasonably priced shoes. Influenced regularly by the catwalk and quick to change stock, you'll always find something to suit a last minute outfit.

MOOD & Singways
JBR The Walk (04 437 6488). **Open** 10am-10pm daily. **Map** p142 B4 ㉕
Two shops in one, Mood sells high end designer gifts and homewares, while Singways is a store that sells high

design inspired goods made in China (the store representative promises they're still of good quality). Also, there's a Paul cafe in store – pastries are always a welcome addition to any shopping experience.

Sconto
Dubai Marina Mall (04 436 1000). **Open** 10am-10pm daily.
Map p142 B5 ㉖
This designer boutique sells sought after labels like Balmain for up to 75 per cent off. Need we say more?

Sunglasses Hut
JBR Walk (04 438 9650). **Open** 10am-midnight daily. **Map** p142 B4 ㉗
This chain is all over the world, but we do find that this branch has particularly quirky designs. From Ray Bans that look like they're crafted from washed up glass to Steve McQueen limited edition Persols, you're sure to find the perfect pair.

Nightlife

Buddha Bar
Grosvenor House (04 399 8888, www.buddha-bar.com) **Open** 6pm-3am daily. **Map** p142 B5 ㉘
Bar-cum-club-cum restaurant that impresses across all three disciplines.

DUBAI BY AREA

The music can border on chin-stroking, but once the bar starts filling up, and the dining gets going, you could be in almost any European city (until the summer heat and humidity hits as you step outside, obviously).

M-Dek

Media One Hotel (04 427 1001, www.mediaonehotel.com). **Open** midday-2am daily. **Map** p142 C5 ㉙
Cool pool bar that doubles as a late night hangout. It's popular with the after-work crowd, and although weekends can be hit and miss, it's normally a good place to start the night after work, especially if you're in the mood for drinks deals.

Tamanya Terrace

Radisson Blu (04 366 9111, www.radissonblu.com/hotel-mediacitydubai). **Open** 6pm-2am daily. **Map** p142 C5 ㉚
A rooftop terrace in the heart of Media City, Tamanya offers impressive views and alfresco dancing outside of the summer months. It's often booked up at weekends with private parties, but if not, it's a good spot to begin or end the night. There's often live music too, worth checking out.

XL Beach Club

Habtoor Grand Resort and Spa (04 408 4444, www.habtoorhotels. com). **Open** midday-3am daily. **Map** p142 B4 ㉛
The latest addition to the beach club scene, XL have set their aims high. And with customised cabanas, butler service and your own bar, it's definitely attracted the bikini and heels and champagne-spraying set at Dubai's Marina.

Arts & leisure

Art Couture Gallery

Al Fattan Marine Towers II, Jumeirah Beach Residence (04 399 4331/www.artcoutureuae. com). **Open** 10am-9pm Sat-Thu; 4pm-9pm Fri. **Map** p142 B4 ㉜
Hosts regular shows, events and a selection of artworks from a global array of artists. Prints, postcards and other art related gifts are also on offer.

Dusail

Dubai Marina (050 551 7280). **Map** p142 A5 ㉝
Morning or sunset cruises are available on the Andorra, a 50ft luxury sailing yacht. All cruises

M-Dek

depart from Dubai International Marine Club and can accommodate up to 15 people. Soft drinks and light snacks are provided.

Grand Megaplex
Ibn Battuta Mall, Jebel Ali (04 366 9898, www.grandcinemas. com). **Open** 10am-midnight daily. **Map** p142 A5 ③④
Offering VIP screens, an IMAX 3D cinema and showing the latest film releases from Hollywood with a selection of Middle Eastern and Indian movies. From Dhs30 per ticket.

Habtoor Grand Resort & Spa Beach Club
Habtoor Grand Resort & Spa, Dubai Marina (04 399 500, www. grandjumeirah.habtoorhotels.com). **Open** 8.30am-7.30pm daily. **Map** p142 B4 ③⑤
This busy beach club features a pool, slide and beach bar, and guests also have full access to a host of watersports activities provided by the Habtoor Grand's privately managed marina and boat charter company, Nautica 1992. Activities include windsurfing (Dhs200 for a lesson), waterskiing (Dhs200 for 20 minutes), wakeboarding (Dhs200 for 20 minutes), banana boating (Dhs250 for a 20-minute ride), and parasailing (Dhs250 for 10-minute flight). Fishing charters are also available. A day pass costs Dhs150 (Sun-Wed); Dhs225 (Thur-Sat).

Hilton Dubai Jumeirah beach club
Dubai Marina (04 399 1111, www.hilton.com). **Open** 9am-6pm daily. **Map** p142 A4 ③⑥
This small but pleasant beach just off The Walk at JBR features a swim-up bar and a baby pool as added bonuses. An array of watersports are provided by Sky & Sea Adventures, which operates out of the Hilton. Options include banana boating (Dhs65 per

Nasimi Beach parties

Dance on the sandy shore to world class DJs

From full moon and foam parties to Faithless gigs and 12-hour music festivals, Nasimi Beach at Atlantis the Palm has seen a phenomenal amount of action since the hotel opened, becoming one of the city's most consistently popular nightspots. Though it closes during summer when temperatures outdoors become inhospitably close to 50°C, for the rest of the year Nasimi hosts the kind of fun-filled beach parties that people look forward to on holiday or when they've decided to make the move abroad. After starting out as a bar and restaurant, the venue began to grow as a nighttime haunt following the launch of its monthly full moon parties (many of them not taking place on an actual full moon, but either the following or preceding weekend), where the city's nocturnal crowd turned up in their beachwear best to party. While many more hotels have since jumped on the beach nightclub bandwagon, few have yet managed to accrue the notoriety of Nasimi. There are themed nights throughout the week, with live DJ sets, plus a ladies' night every Tuesday where the fairer sex can take advantage of selected free drinks. If you're lucky enough to be in town for a party, get there early.
■ Nasimi Beach, Atlantis, The Palm, Palm Jumeirah (055 200 4321).

DUBAI BY AREA

Habtoor Grand Resort & Spa p149

Hilton Dubai Jumeirah p149

person for 15 minutes), and cruises (Dhs200 per person for 30 minutes). Day pass Dhs180 (Sun-Wed); Dhs250 (Thur-Sat).

KO Gym
Dreams building (050 286 1673).
Open 6am-10pm Sun-Thur; 9am-10pm Sat. **Map** p142 A5 ③⑦
Boxing, kickboxing and capoeira are all taught at this Marina-based gym. KO is the driving force behind Dubai's white-collar boxing scene and organises most of the city's boxing and kickboxing events.

N.A.I.L.S Organic Spa
Shop 1, Trident Marinascape, Marina Boulevard, Dubai Marina (04 447 3688, www.nailsorganicspa. com). **Open** 9am-9pm daily. **Map** p142 B5 ③⑧
Organic-only spot that uses fantastic products and offers a great range of fruity treatments. Dhs275-Dhs500 for pretty good facials.

The Ritz-Carlton Beach Club
The Ritz-Carlton, Dubai Marina (04 399 4000, www.ritzcarlton.com). **Open** 9am-6pm daily. **Map** p142 B4 ③⑨
While the Ritz-Carlton doesn't offer any watersports facilities, its private beach is plush. Guests also have access to the spa and fitness facilities, use of tennis and squash courts, plus the Kids Club and kids pool (with slide!). A beac club day pass costs Dhs500 per adult (Dhs150 reductions) and Dhs300 during the week (Dhs75 reductions).

Saray Spa
Dubai Marriott Harbour Hotel & Suites, Al Sufouh Road, Dubai Marina (04 319 4000). **Open** 9am-10pm daily. **Map** p142 B5 ④⓪
A modern spa that features a sleek hammam and uses local products. Massages from Dhs300, facials also from Dhs300.

Sheraton Jumeirah Health & Beach Club
Sheraton Jumeirah Beach Resort & Towers, Dubai Marina (04 399 5533, www.starwoodhotels.com). **Open** 8am-6pm daily. **Map** p142 A4 ④①
While the Sheraton may be one of the older resorts in the Marina area, the beach club is also one of the cheapest in Dubai. Watersports are provided by Sky & Sea Adventures, offering

activities including windsurfing (from Dhs300 per hour), sailing lessons (from Dhs500 per hour), parasailing (from Dhs250 per ride), sport fishing (from Dhs450 for two hours; minimum group of four people), waterskiing (Dhs200 for 15 minutes), and many more. Day pass Dhs100 for adults, Dhs60 for kids (Sun-Thur); Dhs180 for adults, Dhs100 for kids (Fri-Sat).

Skydive Dubai

Opposite Grosvenor House (050 153 3222). **Open** 10am-sunset. **Map** p142 B4 42

Skydive Dubai's aircraft enable you to jump from higher altitudes than most skydiving centres, allowing for more time in freefall. Fall from 13,000ft over the Palm – which from that height actually looks like a Palm, and on a clear day see the Burj Khalifa in the distance. Closed during Ramadan.

Xclusive Yachts

Dubai Marina (04 432 7233, www.xclusiveyachts.com). **Open** 9am-9pm Sun-Thur; 10am-7pm Fri-Sat. **Map** p142 A5 43

This company runs all types of fishing trips on 37ft to 86ft vessels. Dhs2,400 for a four-hour deep-sea fishing trip, equipment and soft drinks included.

The Yellow Boats

Opposite Spinney's, Dubai Marina (800 8044, www.theyellowboats.com). **Map** p142 B5 44

Zip around the Burj Al Arab and Palm Jumeirah area in large 12-seater (yellow) jet boats. The company also offers night-time tours.

The Palm

Sights & museums

The Lost Chambers

Atlantis Palm Jumeirah (04 426 0000, www.atlantisthepalm.com). **Open** 10am-10pm daily.

Admission Dhs75 adults, Dhs50 for children. **Map** p143 D1 45

If you've got a vivid imagination and find the ruins of Atlantis fascinating, you'll fall in love with The Lost Chambers. It's home to 65,000 marine animals including sharks and giant catfish, and invites visitors to live out their own Atlantean adventure through the various underwater halls and tunnels.

Eating & drinking

101

One&Only The Palm (04 440 1010). **Open** 11am-2am daily. **$$$. Bar.** **Map** p142 B2 46

The One&Only The Palm's classy al fresco lounge remains unmatched when it comes to luxurious seclusion. Whether you arrive at the jetty venue by boat from the One&Only Royal Mirage on the main coast or by golf buggy (or foot) from the hotel, you're guaranteed to find the setting impressive. While the prices err on the expensive, and the snack portions on the miniscule, the ambience is incredibly chilled out and the staff simply can't do enough. Perfect for fancy sundowners.

Al Nafoorah

Jumeirah Zabeel Saray (04 453 0444). **Open** 7pm-2am daily. **$$$. Arabic.** **Map** p142 B2 47

A recent 2011 opening, the original Al Nafoorah in Jumeirah Emirates Towers is reputedly a favourite haunt of HRH Sheikh Mohammed Bin Rashid Al Maktoum, ruler of Dubai and vice president of the UAE, so it makes sense that a venue with such star appeal should be replicated.

Amala

Jumeirah Zabeel Saray (04 453 0444). **Open** 2pm-12.30am daily. **$$$. Indian.** **Map** p142 B2 48

Fine dining and slightly OTT Indian. Think regal creams and golds and

DUBAI BY AREA

ornate wrought-iron lamps hang from the ceiling. Yes, it's over the top, but it works. Order as much food as you like from the menu for Dhs225.

Barca

Between Shoreline Apartments nine and 10 (04 439 3548). **Open** 5pm-midnight Sun-Thur; 1pm-midnight Fri-Sat. **$$.** **International**. **Map** p143 D4 (49)

You can choose to chow down on your carbs in either the glamorously bling décor (no doubt decorated to match the former more refined and expensive menu), or outside, on the family-friendly, patio facing the swimming pool and overlooking the beach. In addition to the Italian staples like spaghetti bolognese, penne alfredo and classic pizzas on the menu, there's also something for the Brits – fish and chips and burgers.

Bidi Bondi

Between building 3 and 4, Shoreline apartments (04 427 0515). **Open** 10am-midnight Sun-Thur; 10am-1am Fri-Sat. **$$. Pub**. **Map** p143 D4 (50)

The Palm's ultimate chill-out spot, Bidi's – as it's known to regulars – is the perfect place to unwind during a laid-back afternoon. Whether it's cool enough to bask in the sunshine on the patio overlooking the beach or the heat means you're retiring to a comfy booth indoors, this Aussie bar serves up a wide range of beers and does darn good grub – at far more reasonable prices than many other beachfront bars in the city. Plus they do a mean pub quiz which is always popular and packed.

Lalezar

Jumeirah Zabeel Saray, Palm Jumeirah, Dubai (04 453 0444). **Open** 3pm-6pm, 7pm-11pm Thur-Tue. **$$$. Turkish. Map** p142 B2 (51)

Lalezar markets itself as the city's first Anatolian restaurant, and apparently every tile in this very tiled restaurant has come from Turkey. High end Turkish food really is what's on offer, from kofte to juicy kebabs.

Levantine

Atlantis The Palm (04 426 0000). **Open** 4pm-1.45am Sun-Thur; 2pm-1.45am Fri-Sat. **$$. Middle Eastern. Map** p143 D1 (52)

The restaurant is split between a beautiful terrace and an inside area both accessible by a grand sweeping staircase. For couples and small groups, circular, wind-proof booths are the best bet outside, which feel secluded. Levantine offers Middle Eastern and Lebanese cuisine and has a huge array of starters before a mostly meat-filled (very filling) main course section.

Nasimi

Atlantis The Palm (04 426 0000). **Open** 4pm-11.45pm Sun-Wed; 4pm-1.45am Thur; 1pm-1.45am Fri; 1pm-12.45am Sat. **$$. Bar. Map** p143 D1 (53)

Famed for its fun-fuelled beach soirees and thumping pool parties the year-round (see p155), the fact that Nasimi is also a bar during the week is often overlooked. It shouldn't be. There are few better ways of celebrating the fact you're living or holidaying by the beach, than by having a few mid-week drinks sprawled out on a beanbag with your toes buried in the sand. And even if you're not keen on getting pesky particles where they ought not to be, there's plenty of room indoors to look glam.

Ossiano

Atlantis The Palm (04 426 2626). **Open** 7pm-11.30pm daily. **$$$$. Spanish. Map** p143 D1 (54)

Three time Michelin starred Chef Santi Santamaria's first restaurant outside Spain is a pure delight. Guests are treated like royalty, an attitude that is reflected by the interior design of the restaurant. One wall of the dimly-lit interior is occupied entirely by a huge, calming aquarium.

Wet, wet, wet

Dubai's the place to splash down come summer.

Home to two waterparks – Wild Wadi, next door to the Jumeirah Beach Hotel and Aquaventure, attached to the Atlantis the Palm – Dubai offers more entertaining ways of catching some sun than vegetating on a hotel sun lounger. It's worth noting that like any theme or waterpark, both are often heaving during the weekends, particularly during school holidays (naturally), so the best time to go is first thing on a weekday morning. The older of the two, Wild Wadi, complete with its very own cartoon mascots, recently upped its game with the arrival of two new rides in 2011; the Burj Surj and Tantrum Alley. The park also boasts a permanent wave for aspiring surfers called the flowrider, which projects a flat stream of water up a wave-shaped slope, a wave pool and the infamous Jumeirah Sceirah – a rather high, narrow slide notorious for wedging unwitting sliders' trunks and bikini bottoms much further north than they ought to be. If you feel peckish, there are three restaurants and a number of snack stands around the park for a pit stop.

Over on the Palm Jumeirah, the 42 acre Aquaventure offers adrenalin-filled spurts of action, alongside a rather tame river loop, from which you can hop off and join a queue for one of the tube slides, which will send you shooting off, at points, through near total darkness. Its flagship ride is the Leap of Faith, which consists of a nauseating 27.5m near-vertical drop, that propels the rider at high speed through a clear tunnel through the park's Shark Lagoon. Given the velocity at which you pass through, there's little chance you'll manage to spot one of these scaries, let alone give them a wave, but it's worth joining the queuing troops so you can at least say you've done it.

If you're not in the market for an adrenaline rush, you can try the Shark Attack slide, where you can peer through the safety of an acrylic tunnel, otherwise there's plenty of beach to stretch out on and hundreds of sun loungers and just kick back and relax.

DUBAI BY AREA

Ronda Locatelli

Atlantis The Palm (04 426 2626).
Open noon-3pm, 6pm-10.30pm daily.
$$$. Italian. Map p143 D1 ⑤⑤
Appearances can be deceiving, and the slightly wacky setting for Michelin-star chef Georgio Locatelli's Dubai venture may well raise a few eyebrows among traditionalists, but yell 'bueno sera' and dive in, because the food is anything but tacky. The simplicity of the fresh ingredients leaves diners gasping with delight.

Saffron

Atlantis The Palm (04 426 2626).
Open 7am-noon, 6pm-12.30am daily.
$$$. International. Map p143 D1 ⑤⑥
Head here for a raucous Friday brunch. This international restaurant prides itself on its mammoth range of twenty or so individual food stations, offering everything from Mongolian to French. During a Friday brunch these are joined by multiple drinks stations.

Seafire

Atlantis The Palm (04 426 2626).
Open 6pm-11.30pm daily. **$$$.**
Steakhouse. Map p143 D1 ⑤⑦
Atlantis breeds its own cows in Australia. This means that its corn fed beef literally slides off the knife (the cows have a very nice life) and

for anyone who is concerned about where their food is coming from, proactive steps like this will surely impress. Although a meal here isn't the cheapest, it is a dazzler.

STAY by Yannick Alleno

One&Only The Palm (04 440 1010).
Open 9pm-11pm Tue-Sun. **$$$.**
Modern European. Map p142 B2 ⑤⑧
Not a place for casual dining from three starred Michelin chef Yannick Alleno. Chandeliers swinging down from the impossibly tall ceiling, hung against a backdrop of high timber walls, crisp white tablecloths and suited floor staff fill the floor and there's a far wall entirely dedicated to fragile pastries.

West 14th

Oceana Residence (04 447 7601).
Open noon-3pm, 6pm-midnight daily.
$$$. Steakhouse. Map p143 D3 ⑤⑨
This steakhouse is a welcome addition to the Palm. Guests are left in no doubt as to the restaurant's theme – faux exposed-brick walls and exposed pipes transport diners to the warehouses of New York's Meatpacking District.

Zest

One&Only The Palm (04 440 1010).
Open 7am-11am, 12.30pm-3.30pm,

STAY by Yannick Alleno

7pm-11pm daily. $$$. **International.**
Map p142 B2 ㉚
Zest marries opulence with an
accessible layout and laid-back vibe.
Opt for a table outside so you can look
back on Dubai's twinkling skyline.
The menu offers guests a choice of
West, East or Asian themed food.

Nightlife

Nasimi Beach
*Atlantis (04 426 000, www.atlantis
thepalm.com).* **Open** midday-2am
daily. Map p143 D1 ㉛
A game-changing beach bar since it
opened 2 years ago, Nasimi regularly
draws in over 10,000 clubbers every
weekend who come for the music (the
stand out events being the monthly
Full Moon parties) and to dance on
the sand.

Sanctuary
*Atlantis (04 426 000, www.atlantis
thepalm.com).* **Open** 10pm-3am daily.
Map p143 D1 ㉜
While the main room can lack
atmosphere, this three-roomed
superclub still packs in the punters
thanks to a strong booking policy
and an eclectic choice of music. And
the terrace is one of the best venues in
Dubai in its own right.

Arts & leisure

Al Shalal Beach Club
*Between Shoreline Apartment
buildings Al Nabat and Al Haseer
buildings, 7 and 8.(04 430 9466)*
Open 11am-10pm daily. Map p143
D4 ㉝
Aiming to be the city's most
personalised boutique club, it offers
special events for members, where
they can 'meet and receive guidance
from celebrity and lifestyle gurus'
– joining Al Shalal, it seems, could
make you a new and improved
human being. The infinity pool is
awesome too. What's more, Gusto,

its Mediterranean restaurant, is also
pretty good. Weekly and monthly
passes are available for Dhs500 and
Dhs1,600 respectively, and access to
the pool bar is free.

Aquaventure
*Atlantis Palm Jumeirah (04 426
0000).* **Open** 8am-5pm daily. Map
p143 D1 ㉞
Spread across 42 acres next to
Atlantis, Dubai's newest, steroid-
pumped waterpark sloshes punters
through a series of rapids, waterfalls,
waves and the showpiece slide, the
Leap of Faith. drenaline junkies might
pooh-pooh the river's rapids, which
fling you through caves and chutes;
while they're great for short bursts
of madness, most of the best bits are
followed by rather tame periods of
lazy bobbing.

Atlantis Dive Centre
*Atlantis Palm Jumeirah (04 426
0000).* **Open** 10am-7pm daily. Map
p143 D1 ㉟
Whether you are a beginner or an
established diver, this five-star PADI
Dive Centre has a host of courses to
suit every ability, along with access to
new dive sites along Dubai's coastline
for open-water courses.

SensAsia Urban Spa
Palm Jumeirah (04 422 7115). **Open**
10am-10pm daily. Map p143 D4 ㊱
This fantastic spa features top
massages, blending Balinese,
Japanese and Thai traditions. Best
of all it's not ludicrously expensive.
Massages start from Dhs225.

ShuiQi Spa & Fitness
*Atlantis, Palm Jumeirah
(04 426 1020/www.atlantisthepalm.
com).* **Open** 10am-10pm daily.
Map p143 D1 ㊲
This luxurious spa is home to the
famous Bastien Gonzalez pedicure.
You can also book in for entire day
long rituals for a complete relax.

Qasr Al Sarab Desert Resort p157

Worth the Trip

For many people, the UAE is Dubai. But Dubai's neighbouring emirates have plenty to offer, from forays into the past to futuristic moon-like mountain ranges, engaging insights into Arab and Islamic culture and for the kids, animal and water attractions to satisfy even the grumpiest teenager. Admittedly, the road systems are pretty archaic and public transport is non-existent, but it makes finding these places so much more of an adventure. If you can't rent a car (always go for a 4x4), you'll need to hire a taxi from Dubai Transport (04 208 0808). If you're short on time, go for a half-day desert adventure, which might include dune bashing, quad biking, camel riding, henna painting and a traditional meal. Operators include Arabian Adventures (04 303 4888, www.arabianadventures.com) and Desert Rangers (04 220 0044, www.desertrangers.com) or Absolute Adventure (04 345 9900, www.adventure.ae).

Abu Dhabi

The UAE's capital has a totally different feel to that of its younger sister. An older city centre, with a recognisable grid system where all roads lead to the corniche and wide walkways surround the beachfront, it has both a Mediterranean and Arabian feel. Settled on a series of islands, Abu Dhabi has expanded to now include the developed Yas Island (see p45) and building is still continuing. Come 2012, the capital's Saadiyat Island will be home to new Guggenheim and Louvre museums.

Emirates Palace

Corniche (02 690 7999, www.
emiratespalace.com).
Emirates Palace stands tall over
the waterfront in Abu Dhabi and its
majestic layout inspires you to have
a closer look. Inside, you'll find art
exhibitions as well as sumptuous
restaurants. It's the place for a spot of
afternoon tea. However, reservations
are required and there is a dress code.

Grand Mosque

Between the bridges (800 555).
Open 10am Sat-Thur. **Admission** free.
One of the biggest in the Middle East,
this beautiful specimen of Islamic
architecture features the world's
largest carpet and the world's hugest
chandelier. Tours happen every
day, except Friday, at 10am and
11am. Visitors must remember to be
appropriately dressed and women's
hair must be covered.

Al Ain

Inland, and halfway between Dubai
and Abu Dhabi, lies Al Ain. It's
been inhabited for 4,000 years and
was home to the UAE's founder and
former President, Sheikh Zayed Bin
Sultan Al Nahyan. History buffs
will love the fact it has sites dating
back to the Bronze Age.

Al Ain Wildlife Park & Resort

Al Ain is a 90-minute drive from
Dubai and Abu Dhabi. Once in Al Ain,
follow the brown signs for the Wildlife
Park. (03 782 8188, www.awpr.ae).
Open Sept-Apr 9am-8pm daily, May-
July 4pm-10pm daily. **Admission**
Dhs15, Dhs5 reductions.
In the last few years, the Al Ain
Wildlife Park has spent millions of
dirhams on an enormous conservation
programme. The park is now split into
Arabian, African and Asian areas,
and is home to many rare species.

Compared to other animal attractions
in the UAE, Al Ain actually puts
the animals' welfare first. In the
summer, the park is only open at
night so visitors can view the animals'
nocturnal habits.

Liwa

Liwa sits on the cusp of the Empty
Quarter, the huge rolling desert that
is larger than France, Holland and
Belgium, and separates the UAE
from Saudi Arabia. It was home to
the Bani Yas tribe, founders of Abu
Dhabi. One of the features of this
awe-inspiring space are the 300-
metre high sand dunes.

Qasr Al Sarab Desert Resort by Anantara

Take the E11, then E65 for Hameem.
Turn left onto E90 for 150km until
Hameem. Take second U-turn past the
petrol station, then a right signposted
by the hotel. (02 886 2088, www.
qasralsarab.anantara.com).
Staying at Qasr Al Sarab is one of
the easiest ways to experience the
majesty of the Empty Quarter. The
hotel, which is modelled on an old
traditional fort, can arrange desert
walks, camel treks, archery and
falconry sessions, and more.

Sir Bani Yas Island

Around 8km off the coast from Jebel
Dhanna, which is 240km west of
Abu Dhabi. (02 801 5400, www.
desertislands.anantara.com).
Sir Bani Yas was once former
President, Sheikh Zayed Bin Sultan
Al Nahyan's private island retreat
– it's now an environmentally
friendly resort that aims to nurture
local floral and fauna. There's an
archaeological dig on site which has
unearthed Christian relics and the
island is thought to be 10 million
years old. Accessible by boat or by
plane (from Abu Dhabi), the resort

DUBAI BY AREA

offers a range of outdoorsy pursuits, such as kayaking through mangroves, hiking, snorkeling, nature walks and fascinating safari drives.

Fujairah

Sat on the far east coast just above Oman, Fujairah is a bustling little town that hasn't really embraced the 21st century. For an overnight getaway, it's ideally located.

Fujairah Museum & Fort

At the fish roundabout go inland, take a right at second roundabout and the museum and fort are on the right. **Open** 8am-6.30pm Sat-Thur, 2.30pm-6pm Fri. **Admission** Dhs5.
The fort was built in 1670 and although you can't see inside, it's one of the

better preserved examples of military architecture in the region. Fujairah museum across the road features rock art found in nearby wadis, ancient Islamic coins and Bedouin jewellery.

Hatta

The hidden away mountain town of Hatta offers al fresco swims, wadi bashing and is generally cooler and less humid than lower down Dubai.

Hatta Heritage Village

Take the E44 north out of Dubai. Follow directions for Hatta Fort Hotel, but take the other turning at the roundabout for Heritage Village (04 852 1374). **Open** 9am-sunset daily. **Admission** free.
See life as it was in the 16th century. This traditional Emirati village

Hatta rock pools p159

comprises 30 buildings, including a watch tower and a replica majlis. Slightly freaky dummies occupy the fake village, but this adds some atmosphere at least.

Hatta rock pools
From Hatta head to Jeemah, then Al Tuwayah, then follow a track to the rock pools.
Freshwater pools in the middle of the desert? Perfect for cooling off and picnicking. However, a conservation mindset isn't widespread here so be prepared for litter. Also only accessible with a 4x4 during daylight hours. Nearby Hatta Fort Hotel organises trips if you need help (04 852 3211).

Sharjah

Locals may roll their eyes and groan when this emirate is mentioned, thanks to the permanent traffic jam into Dubai. But this sleepy city, only a few kilometres north of its brash neighbour, has retained more of a traditional feel. It's home to some fantastic museums and art galleries, most centred round the Heritage Area. However, Sharjah is a dry emirate, alcohol is therefore illegal, and visitors should dress more modestly than when in Dubai.

Museum of Islamic Civilisation
Corniche Street, near Radisson Blu (06 565 5455, www.islamicmuseum.ae). **Open** 8am-8pm Sat-Thur, 4pm-8pm Fri. **Admission** Dhs5-10.
This new museum showcases local art from the seventh to 20th century, a collection of rare Arabic manuscripts, and there is also a major Islamic mint exhibition featuring coins from the sixth century. It is also home to a shop, a busy café and a room outlining the Arab world's contribution to science.

Sharjah Art Museum
Al Shuwaiheyn, behind Emirates Post, Rolla district (06 5768 8222). **Open** 9am-1pm, 5pm-8pm Sat-Thur, 5pm-8pm Fri.
A collection from the former ruler of Sharjah makes up a permanent display of 18th and 19th century paintings, while side rooms host well curated rotating exhibitions. The Sharjah Biennial blossoms from here every other year.

Sharjah Old Cars Club & Museum
Next to Sharjah airport, between Interchange 4 and 5 (06 558 0058). **Open** 8am-2pm, 4pm-8pm Sat-Thur, 4pm-8pm Fri.
Cars dating back from 1917 take pride of place in this quirky museum that doubles as a club for classic car enthusiasts. Cars first arrived in Sharjah in 1930, considering the first petrol station didn't open until the '50s, driving then would have been a real adventure.

Ras Al Khaimah

Ras Al Khaimah might look like a sleepy emirate but it's home to a huge array of sports that make the most of its diverse position between the Hajar mountains and the coast.

Ice Land
End of Emirates Road, turn left and park is 4km on the right (800 WOWRAK). **Open** 11am-8pm Sun-Wed, 11am-9pm Fri-Sat. **Admission** Dhs225, Dhs 175 reductions.
We call hundreds of plastic penguins in the desert a sight to behold. Ice Land is the UAE's newest (and certainly largest) water park. It comes complete with a 14-metre waterfall, slides, flumes and a mock shipwreck, water football pitch and more water related activities than you can shake a penguin at.

DUBAI BY AREA

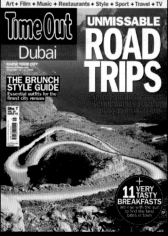

Essentials

Park Hyatt Dubai p164

Hotels

Aquariums, helicopter pads, 63rd-floor bars and gold-plated nightclubs. The world of hotels in Dubai is a heady one. In no other city in the world does the lowly hotel gain superstar status and become an attraction in its own right. But Dubai isn't just any old metropolis. Hotels here aren't only for sleeping in, the entire city's life revolves round five-star hotels. Residents and holidaymakers eat, drink and are merry in the many venues' restaurants, bars and clubs, as these are the only places permitted to hold alcohol licenses. From a leisurely brunch at the Ritz to sundowners on the terrace at the Westin, or dancing the night away at Armani hotel's club Privé – if you want to get the best out of Dubai, you'd best know your hotels. The city is also home to some of the most iconic hotels of recent years, from the sail-shaped Burj Al Arab to the tallest building in the world, Burj Khalifa, all have played a part in creating the Dubai we know today. The options for where to stay can feel endless so this section has rounded up the best hotels, by area, and across various different budgets.

Location, location, location

As with all cities, prices vary depending on which part of town you're in. Generally the nearer the beach, Downtown or the new Marina area you are, the more you can expect to pay. Older parts of Dubai, such as Deira and Bur Dubai, will cost less, but you'll spend more in taxis and the difference between facilities of hotels in the same street can be huge. However, if you want a slice of Middle Eastern culture, Old Dubai is where to find it, with bustling streets and exotic souks. For those that want a beach holiday – head to Jumeirah, the Palm or the Marina – many hotels have their own private beach and offer a range of watersports. For those that want to indulge in Dubai's infamous shopping malls, the new Downtown area is home to The Dubai Mall – the largest mall in the world – it has become a hub for those that are after the latest designer wardrobe.

Thankfully, budget hotels have started to spring up as well – most noticeably in Al Barsha, the area around Mall of the Emirates. These are much handier and have better facilities than the ones located across the Creek (see p167 for more).

Prices

Rates vary hugely in Dubai, most dip substantially over the hot summer season (June-September) and then dip some more during Ramadan. Our ratings are based on the hotel's own prices. By booking through an online broker or an airline like Emirates, cheaper deals and multi-night stays are common. All hotels are subject to 10 per cent tax and 10 per cent municipality fee – make sure that your final rate includes these two. The hotels are divided into four categories, according to the price for a one night's stay in a double room with a shower/bath: $ Dhs499 and under; $$ Dhs500-999; $$$ Dhs1,000-1,499; $$$$ Dhs1,500 and above.

Deira

Al Mamzar Apartments
Sharjah border (04 297 2921). **$.**
Great for an out of town experience. Head down to Al Mamzar beach park, which offers acres of space for

---

S H O R T L I S T

For spotting a footballer
- Atlantis (see p174)
- Le Royal Meridien (see p173)

For watersports
- Le Meridien Mina Seyahi Beach Resort & Spa (see p173)

For a beach bar
- Hilton Jumeirah (see p173)
- The Westin (see p174)

For romance
- Burj Al Arab (see p172)
- Jumeirah Zabeel Saray (see p174)

For souks
- Hilton Dubai Creek (see p164)

For a waterpark
- Jumeirah Beach Hotel (see p172)

For a cheap stay
- Citymax (see p171)
- Holiday Inn (see p171)

For shopping
- The Address Dubai Mall (see p168)

For business
- Radisson Downtown (see p169)

---

ball games, plenty of shade for the barbecue and proper waves. However roads in and out of Sharjah are often gridlocked.

Dubai Youth Hostel
Ousais Road, nr Al Mulla Plaza (04 298 8161, www.uaeyha.com).
No credit cards. **$.**
Youth hostels are rare things in a city full of bling and big bank balances.

Even though this place is pretty basic accommodation-wise, it's popular for budget reasons and it has options of family rooms, singles and doubles. It just wouldn't be Dubai unless the hostel had a pool, gym, Jacuzzi, spa, sauna and a tennis court. Be warned though, this is pretty far out of town, so be prepared to spend on taxis.

Hilton Dubai Creek
Baniyas Road (04 227 1111, www.hiltonworldresorts.com). **$$**.
For a touch of Old Dubai, the Hilton offers a five-class stay next to the Creek in the bustling area of Deira. Although it's away from its peers in Downtown and New Dubai, if you want more culture than shopping, Deira's not a bad place to base yourself. Fine dining lovers must visit Gordon Ramsay's Verre, the first celebrity chef restaurant in the city. For a cheaper experience, the same culinary team also head up brasserie Glasshouse.

JW Marriott Hotel Dubai
Muraqqabat Street (04 262 4444, www.jwmarriott.com). **$$$**.
Old world charm and class simmer away quietly at the JW Marriot, which is like a stately uncle to the new

hotels' teenage kicks. It is also home to JW Marriott's Steakhouse, where you'll find leather armchairs, a quiet ambience and huge portions. The brand's signature beds will ensure you get a good night's sleep.

Park Hyatt Dubai
Dubai Creek Golf & Yacht Club (04 602 1234, www.dubai.park.hyatt.com). **$$$**.
Proving that it's not all about how tall you can build it, the Park Hyatt is one of the city's most stunning hotels. It's full of low slung, white Moroccan architecture with a criss-cross of glass enclosed paths winding through landscaped gardens. It's also home to award-winning French restaurant Traiteur, and is the perfect place to people watch (Elle Macpherson, Giorgio Armani and Tommy Hilfiger have all been spotted).

Radisson SAS Hotel
Deira Creek Baniyas Road (04 222 7171, www.radissonsas.com). **$$**.
Almost as old as the UAE itself, this '70s monolith was Dubai's first five-star hotel. Impeccable service, brilliant restaurants and interesting decor still make the Radisson SAS (formerly known as the InterContinental) a fine

InterContinental Festival City p165

place to stay, but you can't escape the feeling that time has taken its toll.

Sheraton Dubai Creek
Baniyas Road (04 228 1111, www.sheraton.com/dubai). **$$**.
Although there's nothing wrong with this hotel, plenty more have opened up with better options and in better locations. Although you're near the airport, the rest of the city has moved south, so it can feel a little empty with the ghosts of guests past. Still, it's good value for money and Ashiana, the Indian restaurant is excellent.

Sun & Sand Hotel
Nr Dubai Clock Tower, off Maktoum Road (04 223 9000). **$$**.
One of the better options in the area, this small, reasonably well-equipped hotel includes a pool, gym and shuttle services to the shopping malls, airport and beach. Don't be fooled by the name though, you're some way from the shore (although there is a rooftop swimming pool). The decor is dated (think in the vein of gilt-edged sofas and marble floors), but the amenities are fair and the staff are friendly.

Garhoud

Le Méridien Dubai
Airport Road (04 282 4040, www.lemeridien.com). **$$$**.
The beauty of Le Méridien lies not in its decor (faded florals and chintz), but in its location, next to the airport. The hotel also benefits from the huge array of bars and restaurants in the 'Village' attached. From al fresco dining in pretty little gardens to sipping on cocktails at wine bar The Warehouse – the complex is always busy come evening. It's also the location for Dubai's wildest brunch at Yalumba.

Millennium Airport Hotel
Casablanca Road (04 282 3464, www.millenniumhotels.com). **$$**.

As you'd expect from the name, this comfortable address is within spitting distance of Dubai's main airport terminal, so attracts suits and airline crew. Muzak aside, the marble-heavy hotel foyer is elegant and the large pool and banks of green grass make it a family favourite. Rooms are large, airy and have pleasant garden views.

Festival City

Crowne Plaza Festival City
Dubai Festival City (04 701 2222, www.dubaihotels.crowne plaza.com). **$$**.
Sitting alongside the banks of Dubai Creek, Crowne Plaza is geared for those who want to hit the nearby fairways and the adjacent shopping mall. Sat next door to the slightly more expensive InterContinental, the hotel houses the Belgian Beer Café – a pleasant gastropub with a fab terrace to sink a pint and watch the sun set over Dubai's skyline.

InterContinental Festival City
Dubai Festival City (04 701 1111, www.ichotelsgroup.com). **$$**
Rooms here have mastered the art of being homely, with knick-knacks and vases adding a nice touch. It's also home to *Time Out's* 2011 Restaurant of the Year, Reflets par Pierre Gagnaire. While it isn't the busiest restaurant in the world, it is a must-experience. Although not in the centre of town, Festival City is near the airport and has everything a short stopover might need.

Bur Dubai

Arabian Courtyard Hotel
Al Fahidi Street, opposite Dubai Museum (04 351 9111, www.arabian courtyard.com). **$$**.
This new-to-look-like-old hotel runs with the whole Arabian theme, think heavy wood and plenty of gold curtains in spacious rooms, all in all

XVA p167

a comfortable option. The restaurant and bar options tend to be a little hit and miss, but for exploring Old Dubai you couldn't ask for a better location. Ask for a room with Creek views.

Ascot Hotel
Khalid Bin Waleed Road (04 352 0900, www.ascothoteldubai.com). $$.
The Ascot's a lively sort of place, especially if you're looking for middle-aged expats who've been in town a while. Long suffering, but ultimately friendly staff ensure this place ticks over. Although it has a grand façade, the rather dated interior means you might be disappointed if you book this off the web. Popular Irish pub Waxy's though has mastered the art of helping you forget.

Dhow Palace Hotel
Kuwait Street (04 359 9992, www.dhowpalacehoteldubai.com). $$.
Taking the name literally, the building is shaped like a ship, the staff wear nautical uniforms and there's a club in the basement called Submarine,

shaped like… a submarine. As kitsch as it seems, if you're after three-star luxury in Bur Dubai, the Dhow is your best bet. It's also home to the top Indian restaurant in town, Aangan, and it won't cost the earth.

Four Points by Sheraton
Khalid bin Walid Street (04 397 7444, www.fourpoints.com/burdubai). $$.
Just looking for a place to sleep, shower and use the internet? Four Points doesn't offer a lot more than that but it's clean, quiet and the staff are on the ball. Geared towards business visitors rather than pleasure seekers, it might disappoint some looking for luxury.

Majestic Hotel Tower
Mankhool Road (04 359 8888, www.dubaimajestic.com). $$.
The Majestic is one of the better options in Bur Dubai, which is handy for the historical Bastakiya area, full of independent art galleries. The hotel is home to one of the best live music venues in town, The Music Room. Rooms are a decent size and suites

music venues in town, The Music Room. Rooms are a decent size and suites have floor-to-ceiling windows. For the area, the pool deck is pretty good too.

XVA

Al Fahidi roundabout, Bastakiya, behind Basta Art Café (04 353 5383). **$$**.
Is it a hotel, café or gallery? XVA is all three and also Dubai's only boutique-boho hotel. Set in the cultural area of Bastakiya, this 70-year-old Arabic house has been restored, with each room inspired and decorated by local artists. Although facilities are basic (don't expect to find a TV here), the setting's unique and you'll meet a range of interesting people at breakfast in the courtyard each day.

Oud Metha

Arabian Park Hotel

Nr Wafi City, opposite Grand Hyatt Dubai (04 324 5999, www. arabianparkhoteldubai.com). **$**.
A modern three-star hotel, rooms are adequate for what you're paying and if you book a room on one of the top floors, you at least get a view. Breakfast is included in the Executive Rooms, the hotel has a decent pool and offers free airport transfers. If you're looking to save money, you could do a lot worse.

Grand Hyatt

Qataiyat Road (04 317 1234, www.dubai.grand.hyatt.com). **$$$**.
Fourteen restaurants, landscaped gardens, three pools, a running track, a spa and an indoor rainforest will ensure that young 'uns will be stimulated. Although slightly older now, rooms are on the large side and decorated in (surprisingly) subtle Arabic style with views of the historic Dubai Creek. In case you need something more gaudy, the Egyptian-themed shopping mall, Wafi, is next door.

Budget not bling

Dubai's hotel options are more varied than ever.

In the past if you didn't want to drop several thousand dirhams on a hot holiday hotel, your alternative options were limited to a youth hostel halfway out of town, some pretty dodgy hotels in Bur Dubai, frequented by people with questionable morals, or not even getting on a plane. But with the development in different mid-town areas, Al Barsha particularly (a residential area around Mall of the Emirates), decent three or four star hotels, such as Holiday Inn (p171) and Citymax (p171) have sprung up – offering modern, clean, airport style hotel rooms for around Dhs250 a night or less. Al Barsha is also walking distance (except in the summer months) to the Metro which runs the length of Dubai, making it cheap and convenient to hit all the malls for under Dhs20. The area's littered with fantastic Lebanese restaurants where a meal won't cost the earth too. Other areas that have seen a rise in reasonable hotels are Dubai Knowledge Village and Garhoud (both Holiday Inns). For holiday makers who intend on spending more time in malls, bars and on the beach than a hotel room, sacrifice the private butler and Jacuzzi for a place to just sleep and shower. It'll leave you more money to spend on enjoying yourself, rather than the fear of bankruptcy every time you open the mini bar.

Mövenpick Hotel Bur Dubai

19th Street, Oud Metha (04 336 6000, www.moevenpick-burdubai.com). **$$**.

Not a hotel or a location you'd immediately leap to book, the Mövenpick is actually one of the better options in its price range. Although room views are lacking, the rooftop pool is a relaxing place to hang out and bedrooms are surprisingly modern, spacious and clean. Al Nasr Leisureland over the road has tennis courts, an ice rink and a bowling alley.

Raffles Dubai

Oud Metha (04 324 8888 www.dubai.raffles.com). **$$$$**.

Although it's shaped like an Egyptian pyramid and the themed marble lobby might put off some, it's actually a lot more tasteful than it sounds. A wow hotel without being totally bling, the hotel's al fresco garden is one of the quietest spots in the city, while new bar RED Lounge at the apex affords spectacular views.

Ibis World Trade Centre Dubai

Behind World Trade Centre (04 318 7000, www.ibishotel.com). **$**.

For visitors to the city on business, especially for one of the constant stream of exhibitions and conferences, the Ibis is a reasonable three-star stay. There's no pool and the rooms are small, but if a bed's all you need, it'll more than suffice.

Jumeirah Emirates Towers

Opposite The Gate, DIFC (04 330 0000, www.jumeirahemiratestowers.com). **$$$$**.

This iconic pair of towers has dominated the lower part of Sheikh Zayed Road for the last two decades. Elegant and opulent, the large lobby is home to plenty of meetings, while the glass lifts whizz up and down the 52 stories. Suites feature a large separate living/working room and bedroom, with views over DIFC.

The Ritz-Carlton, DIFC

DIFC, (04 372 2222, www.ritzcarlton.com). **$$$$**.

A newcomer to the Downtown area is this city-chic style retreat, hidden away in DIFC. Subtle European grandeur and exemplary service bring the famous brand to life, while the spa offers a popular range of express treatments for jetsetters. The suites each feature a huge marble bathtub and separate living area.

The Address Downtown

Downtown Dubai (04 436 8888, www.theaddress.com). **$$$$**.

The first Address hotel to open in Dubai is also the most lush. It's sail-like appearance seems dwarfed by the next door Burj Khalifa, but it's a fabulous hotel in its own right. The tiered infinity pool, which is right next to The Dubai Mall and the Dubai Fountains, is one of the places to be seen, as is the 63rd floor black-marbled cocktail bar Neos. Rich fabrics and quality furnishings make this a sumptuous, but not OTT, place to stay.

The Address Dubai Mall

Downtown Dubai (04 4 438 8888, www.theaddress.com). **$$$$**.

You can't get any closer to the action then staying in the hotel attached to The Dubai Mall. Without even leaving the building you can go ice-skating, dive with sharks, watch the largest fountains in the world and of course, hit the stores. Although the hotel only has one restaurant, Ember, the rooms are suitably luxurious.

Al Manzil Hotel

Emaar Boulevard, Downtown (04 428 5888, www.almanzilhotel.com). **$$**.

Jumeirah Emirates Towers p168

Sat opposite The Palace is Al Manzil, a slightly less decadent option right at the centre of Dubai's new area. The Dubai Mall is on your doorstep, while rooms are large and feature open bathrooms with a rainfall shower and a bath large enough to sink a battleship, complete with its own plasma telly.

Al Murooj Rotana Hotel & Suites Dubai
Al Saffa Street, off Sheikh Zayed Road (04 321 1111, www.almuroojrotana hoteldubai.com). **$$**
For the last two years, the Al Murooj has disappeared behind a maze of construction for The Dubai Mall and Burj Khalifa, but it's slowly re-emerging. A family hotel with a less modern feel than those across the road in Downtown, book rooms higher up than the second floor to escape the noise. Also home to the rather rowdy Double Decker pub which regularly shows live sport action.

Armani Hotel
Burj Khalifa, Downtown (800 ARMANI, www.armanihotels.com). **$$$$**.

Giorgio Armani's first foray into hospitality had to be based in the world's tallest building didn't it? Muted browns and cream deck out this bizarrely laid out hotel, as it squeezes itself into the bud-shaped lower levels of the Burj. For amazing Downtown views and an enviable address, look no further. If your pockets aren't bottomless, then you might want to think again.

The Palace
Emaar Boulevard, Downtown (04 428 7888, www.theaddress.com). **$$$$**.
Now one of the jewels in the Downtown area, The Palace is an Arabic-inspired resort in the shadow of the Burj Khalifa. Seriously decadent, the entrance way curves round a reflective pool, which is even more impressive after dark. Both the spa and the signature restaurants have become hits with residents.

Radisson Blu, Downtown
Downtown Dubai (04 450 2000 www.radissonblu.com). **$$**.
One of the newest hotels to open in Downtown, the Radisson offers those who aren't millionaires a chance to stay at the centre of the city. Five minutes from Downtown's sights and happily all rooms have free Wi-Fi.

Sheikh Zayed Road

Crowne Plaza Hotel Dubai
Off Trade Centre roundabout, next to The Fairmont (04 331 1111, www. ichotels.com). **$$$**.
One of the first hotels to open in Dubai, the Crowne Plaza is relatively low to the ground compared to the skyscrapers that now surround it. Although the rooms need a refresh and are small by today's standards, it has a central location and plenty of pubs and restaurants dotted throughout its own complex and within walking distance. Bar Trader Vic's is bsuy every night of the week.

ESSENTIALS

Dusit Dubai

Near DIFC Metro station (04 343 3333, www.dusit.com). $$.

Built to resemble hands in a Thai prayer, this Eastern chain is easy to forget among the newer, louder hotels, but it shouldn't be overlooked. Asian chic dominates throughout and rooms have fantastic views over the new Downtown area. Previously in the middle of the conversion of Defence roundabout into a small Spaghetti Junction, the Dusit has emerged intact. Handy for anyone with an interest in the world's largest mall, just five minutes away.

Fairmont Dubai

Sheikh Zayed Road, off Trade Centre roundabout next to Crowne Plaza (04 332 5555, www.fairmont.com). $$$.

At night, the Fairmont's multicoloured hue makes it a landmark for Sheikh Zayed Road. Inside, it's simple luxury, with a graceful lobby and fantastic international restaurant Spectrum on One, on the first floor. Rooms are generous, light and airy. The Fairmont's also home to designer Roberto Cavalli's suitably OTT restaurant-cum-club, Cavalli Club and perenially popular The 400 Club, so named for its capacity.

The Monarch Dubai

Trade Centre roundabout (04 501 8888, www.themonarchdubai.com). $$$$.

Standing at One Sheikh Zayed Road is this five-star hotel, geared up for business visitors to the World Trade Centre over the road. Having said that, the spa here is excellent, especially for express treatments and the Japanese restaurant Okku, is one of the best in the city. Guests with wads of cash can reserve the Sky Suite, which is literally suspended between two towers, and then book a table at the 24-carat gold-plated club below, imaginatively titled, Gold.

Towers Rotana

Sheikh Zayed Road (04 343 8000 www.rotana.com). $$

Part of the well-known Middle Eastern chain, this skyscraper property is a great mid-range stay for those that aren't into over-the-top fuss. Rooms come with brightly-coloured furnishings and although there's an outside pool and Jacuzzi, beach access will cost you extra. International dining restaurant Teatro is popular locally, while basement bar Long's channels some UK boozer charm.

Satwa

Jumeirah Rotana Dubai

Al Dhiyafah Road, Satwa (04 345 5888, www.rotana.com). $$.

Slightly misleading, this hotel is actually in Satwa, a bustling locally populated area set back from the sea. But for a reasonable three-star hotel, where you won't feel underdressed if you're not wearing this season's catwalk, the Rotana is a solid choice. A rooftop pool, kids pool and gym are available, while rooms are light and large.

Rydges Plaza

Al Diyafah Street Satwa (04 398 2222, www.rydges.com). $.

Rydges is in an older part of town that is lacking in other hotels, beaches and designer malls, but it makes up for it with local character. Rooms are have a combination of dark wood furnishings with chintz patterned beds that should have been left behind in the '80s. The hotel's undergoing rejuvenation and rooms now feature 'Dream Beds', made by Australia's oldest bed manufacturer.

Jumeirah

Dubai Marine Beach Resort & Spa

Jumeirah Beach Road, Jumeirah (04 346 1111, www.dxbmarine.com). $$$$.

A low-rise hotel is rare in town, but the older Dubai Marine Beach Resort is one of the finest chill out spots you can find. Thirty three villa-style buildings are set in attractive, lush grounds, with several pools and it's right next to a stretch of private beach. There is also a healthy collection of *Time Out*-awarded bars and clubs.

Al Barsha

Citymax

Mall of the Emirates (04 409 8000, www.citymaxhotels.com) **$**.
Cheap, cheerful but modern and clean, Citymax is the choice of many residents for sending visitors to. Rooms come with flat screen TVs, kettles and fridges and either a bath or shower. There's a 24-hour café, sports bar and restaurant, all of which offer reasonably priced food. The hotel does charge for Wi-Fi, however.

Holiday Inn Express

Sheikh Zayed Road (04 3234333, www. holidayinn.com/hotels/us/en/dubai). **$**.
A seven-storey solid budget offering, Holiday Inn Express is a few minutes walk to Mall of the Emirates and home to a fantastic Thai restaurant that is well-priced. Pick up free Wi-Fi in the lobby or head up to the rooftop pool for views of the Burj Al Arab.

Kempinski Hotel Mall of the Emirates

Mall of the Emirates, Al Barsha Interchange (04 341 0000, www.kempinski.com). **$$$$**.
Kempinski is part of Mall of the Emirates, the now only second largest mall in the UAE, but still the only one with an indoor ski slope. Shop, snowboard, snuggle up with a hot chocolate and go swimming in the hotel's rooftop pool, all without leaving the one building. Some of the best pizzas in town are served in Après next door.

The Pullman

Mall of the Emirates (04 437 72000, www.pullmanhotels.com). **$$**.
The Kempinski's younger, trendier (cheaper) sister hotel, The Pullman opened in 2010 at the other end of Mall of the Emirates. Its poolside wine bar Vintage has a great selection, while

Kempinski Hotel Mall of the Emirates

ESSENTIALS

Al Qasr

the all-day dining restaurant Sanabel has attracted new fans. Rooms are modern, fresh and feature up-to-date technology. A good base for people wanting to explore New Dubai and the Palm.

Umm Suqeim

Al Qasr
Al Sufouh Road (04 366 8888, www.madinatjumeirah.com). $$$$.
Al Qasr builds on the decadence started at Mina A'Salam next door, and channels as much Arabic hospitality as it can cram in, between traditional lanterns, cushions and a 24-hour butler service. The hotel's supported by a fabulous cigar lounge and the trendy Bahri bar, which affords picture postcard views over the Burj Al Arab next door.

Burj Al Arab
Off Jumeirah Beach Road (04 301 7777, www.burj-al-arab.com). $$$$.
The only hotel in the world that reckons it's seven stars is nothing if not extravagant. The iconic building's sail stands proud on its own man-made island and if you're not staying here, then reservations are

compulsory to even enter the grounds. If you want to drop in via helicopter instead it has its own landing pad, 200 metres above the ground. Gold, bling, waterfalls and more gold adorn the hotel; subtlety is an art not yet discovered here.

Jumeirah Beach Hotel
Jumeirah Beach Road (04 348 0000, www.jumeirahbeachhotel.com). $$$$.
Sitting in the shadow of the Burj Al Arab, Jumeirah Beach Hotel is a huge family-centred resort, which is remarkably laid back considering its neighbour. A private beach, plenty of watersports on offer, kids club and five outdoor pools mean there's plenty to do. Kids will love the Wild Wadi waterpark next door, while you'll love 360 – an alfresco bar in the ocean with killer views.

Mina A'Salam
Al Sufouh Road (04 366 8888, www.madinatjumeirah.com). $$$$.
Palatial luxury at the Madinat Jumeirah complex, which combines (faux) souks, restaurants and bars alongside three hotels. Use the Venetian-style canals and dhow boats to traverse from hotel to restaurant

and back again, and embrace Dubai's rather over the top opulence.

One&Only Royal Mirage

Al Sufouh Road (04 399 9999, www.oneandonlyresorts.com). $$$$.
Hidden away next to the actual royal palace, the Royal Mirage is a peaceful oasis of luxury with three separate residences, all modelled on an Arabian fort, which offer indulgent levels of hospitality. Quiet, serene but endlessly accommodating, staff here will really make you feel on top of the world. Head to new beach bar Jetty Lounge if you need a top up of Dubai's party people.

Marina

The Address Dubai Marina

Dubai Marina (04 436 7777, www. theaddress.com/en/hotel/dubai-marina). $$.
For shopaholics, you can't get much closer to Dubai Marina Mall than this. The Address hotels offer chic, five-star luxury but tend to be functional also. This hotel features an infinity pool overlooking Dubai Marina and bustling cocktail bar Blends, popular with local girls and boys around town.

Grosvenor House

West Marina Beach (04 399 8888, www.starwoodhotels.com). $$$$.
Although it has the cache of being a five-star hotel, with skyhigh bars and restaurants to match, including the famous Buddha Bar, Grosvenor House suffers from a lack of beach access and a lot of nearby construction. However, guests can use the beach facilities at the Royal Méridien down the road.

Habtoor Grand Resort & Spa

Al Sufouh Road (04 399 5000. www. grandjumeirah.habtoorhotels.com). $$$$.
The Habtoor's nothing if not luxurious, but it's the kind of ostentatious luxury that can look dated easily. Although there are more extravagant hotels, you'll need to pack some serious designer clothes and heels if you want to fit in among the road-scraping Ferraris that pull up here. Pools, a private beach, plenty of restaurants and activities mean this is a full on beach resort experience complete with weekend beach parties and ladies' nights, five star steakhouses and more.

Hilton Dubai Jumeirah

Al Sufouh Road (04 399 1111, www.hiltonworldresorts.com). $$$$.
A classic resort hotel, this is more of a package deal holiday rather than a luxury destination. It's also now looking quite tired compared to all the new hotels that have popped up on its doorstep. Decent-sized rooms are comfortable and functional, with private little balconies that offer views across the Gulf. Hidden behind the pool terrace is Wavebreakers, a casual, fun beach bar with a pool table.

Le Méridien Mina Seyahi Beach Resort & Marina

Al Sufouh Road (04 399 3333, www. lemeridien-minaseyahi.com). $$$$.
If you're after a beach, look no further. It has one of the largest sand strips in town at 850m, plenty of room for you to stretch out the sun lounger. Balconies overlook the Palm, but be make sure to ask for one when you book. The hotel's also home to the infamous beach bar Barasti so nights could be noisy.

Le Royal Méridien

Al Sufouh Road (04 399 5555, www.leroyalmeridien-dubai.com). $$$$.
Opulence is the name of the game here, as the Royal Méridien is a step up from its sister hotel above. Beautiful, landscaped gardens are overlooked

by a variety of rooms and suites which go for a classic style rather than ultra-modern. Also home to the *Time Out* award-winning, Maya, for contemporary Latin American food. Check out Bar Below for a drink.

Mövenpick JBR

The Walk, Dubai Marina (04 449 8888, www.moevenpick-hotels.com). **$$**.
Spacious, comfortable rooms belie the fact that this hotel is on the doorstep of the Walk, the bustling centre of Dubai Marina. You're right opposite a public beach and the poolside bar straddles the street below. Internet access is pricey here, so upgrade to an Executive Room to get it thrown in.

The Ritz-Carlton, Dubai

The Walk, Dubai Marina (04 399 4000, www.ritzcarlton.com). **$$$$**.
Standards are always high at The Ritz. Try booking rooms at the Club Level, where you can enjoy breakfast, hors d'oeuvres, cocktails and loads of goodies all through the day at the Club Lounge for free (it's included in the room rate). The hotel is going through an expansion so there might be some disruption. Although it's one of a few Marina hotels with a private beach, you'll pay for the privilege.

Sofitel JBR

The Walk, Dubai Marina (04 4 448 4848, www.sofitel.com). **$$**.
A cheaper but modern option for a Marina-based hotel, Sofitel's a solid four-star stay, with a outside pool (and pool bar) that sits back from the beach. Rooms should be booked on a higher floor so you can see the sparkling Arabian Gulf.

Westin Dubai Mina Seyahi Beach Resort & Marina

Al Sufouh Road (04 399 4141, www.westin.com/dubaiminaseyahi). **$$$$**.
Grand and elegant, the Westin is impressive on first arrival, with a large marble lobby and several swimming pools. However, the roads around it are a hotch-potch of construction, so don't expect to go walking outside the resort once you've unpacked. Check out Bussola, *Time Out's* favourite (alfresco) Italian, two years in a row for amazing pizzas and more classy dishes.

The Palm

Atlantis

The Palm (04 426 1000, www. atlantisthepalm.com). **$$$$**.
The hotel behemoth houses 1,500 rooms and suites and is gaudily based around the lost island of Atlantis. Cue huge aquariums, a 40-acre water park and a dolphin bay. Really only advisable with kids in tow, although it's also home to Dubai's Nobu.

Jumeirah Zabeel Saray

The Palm (04 364 7555, www.jumeirah. com). **$$$**.
The architects behind Zabeel Saray have been inspired by the Ottoman Empire. Rooms and suites are as luxurious as it gets and there are some new dining experiences (and we do mean experiences) to be had here such as Al Nafoorah for Lebanese cuisine (make sure you order the mezze) and Amala for high-end Indian fare.

One&Only The Palm

The Palm (04 440 1010, www.thepalm. oneandonlyresorts.com) **$$$$**.
This recent opening in Dubai has upped the style stakes. A desert island-feel invades the resort, while beach bar 101 channels St Tropez charm effortlessly. Quiet, sheltered and secluded guest suites means this place is a haven for honeymooners and you'll often spot loved-up celebs. Chef Yannick Alléno has also just opened contemporary European restaurant STAY, here. Head to 101 for drinks before getting a speedboat to the sister hotel on the mainland.

Getting Around

Airport

Dubai International Airport

(04 224 5555, www.dubaiairport.com, for flight enquiries call 04 216 6666). One of the most highly acclaimed airports in the world, it boasts three terminals, one exclusively for Emirates airline flights (Terminal 3). Almost all other major airlines arrive at Terminal 1. Here, Dubai Duty Free (800 4443) is the last port of call for the purchase of alcohol before entering Dubai's 'hotel only' licensing restrictions. Airport facilities include internet and banking services, shops, restaurants, business services, a bar, a hotel and a regular raffle that gives you the chance to win a luxury car. Raffle tickets cost Dhs500, but odds are favourable as there is a draw every time 1,000 are sold. The smaller Terminal 2 caters largely for charter flights, cargo, and commercial airlines to Iran and the CIS countries. Local budget airline Flydubai tends to fly fromTerminal 2. There is also a VIP terminal, which is known as Al Majlis. A card-operated system enables residents who carry the relevant smart card to check in and travel unhindered, using nothing more than their fingerprints for identification. For more information, see the airport website. For a fee of about Dhs100, the Marhaba welcome service will usher you from the plane to taxi and ease you though immigration.
For more information, visit www.marhabameetandgreet.com.

To & from the airport

Dubai International Airport is in Garhoud, about five kilometres (three miles) south-east of the city centre. If you're staying at an international hotel, you'll likely get a complimentary shuttle bus or limousine transfer to and from the airport. Otherwise, taxis are the most convenient and practical form of transport. There is a Dhs20 surcharge on pick-up from the terminal (instead of the usual minimum fare of Dhs10). This means that the journey from the airport to the city centre costs around Dhs50, while the return journey is Dhs25 or so. It takes about 10 minutes to travel to Bur Dubai, Jumeirah, and the hotel beach resorts are about half an hour away. There are bus links to and from both terminals every 20 or 30 minutes for less than Dhs3, although you can't get on without a Nol card (used on the Dubai Metro and other public transportation, but not taxis) – you can pick one up from any Metro station in the city. All buses and several major bus stops around town are air conditioned, so you won't be left standing in sweltering summer heat. Call 04 227 3840, 800 9090 or see www.rta.ae for public transportation routes, timings and other details.

Airport parking

There are short- and long-term car parking facilities at the airport. Tariffs range from Dhs10 per hour in the short-stay car park, to Dhs120 per day for up to 10 days in the long-stay area.

Airlines

All airlines operating regular flights into Dubai are listed on the airport website; some of the most popular are listed below. Note that some airlines ask you to reconfirm your flight 72 hours before departure and that cheaper tickets will often incur a penalty fee for alteration or cancellation.

Air France *04 602 5400, www.airfrance.ae*
British Airways *04 307 5777, 8000 441 3322, www.britishairways.com*
Emirates *04 214 4444, www.emirates.com*
Etihad Airways *02 511 0000, www.etihadairways.com*
Gulf Air *04 316 6442, 04 216 2730, www.gulfair.com*
KLM *800 4555, www.klm.com*
Lufthansa *04 216 6855, www.lufthansa.com*
Qatar Airways *04 229 2229, www.qatarairways.com*
Royal Brunei (No alcohol served on board) *04 351 4111, www.bruneiair.com*

By sea

There are boats to Dubai from Iraq and Iran; journey time is more than two days for around Dhs580 return. For schedules and details contact the Dubai Ports Authority (04 881 5555/www.dpa.co.ae).

By road

The UAE is bordered to the north and east by Oman, and to the south and west by Saudi Arabia. Road access to Dubai is via the Abu Dhabi emirate to the south, Sharjah and Ajman to the north, and Oman to the east. There is no charge for driving or border between the seven emirates, but travel to or from Oman or Saudi Arabia requires your passport, a valid driving licence, insurance and a visa. Crossing the Oman border costs Dhs35 first to receive a UAE exit stamp on your passport, and then an additional Dhs30 (OMR 3) if you have UAE

residency or Dhs60 (OMR 6) for those on a visit visa.

Check www.rop.gov.om for the latest visa requirements before you leave. Your car will be searched and remember that carrying alcohol is prohibited. All the highways linking Dubai to other emirates and Oman are in good condition. Ensure that your vehicle and the air-conditioning are in working order, as it is inevitably hot and the drive through the Hajar Mountains to Muscat, Oman's capital, takes around five hours. Check with Immigration (04 216 2388) before you leave for any changes in local travel policies.

Due to the intense heat and humidity, an outdoor stroll is unpleasant between May and September, and certain areas in the city lack pavements. In pleasant weather, the best places for a walk include the Creek-side areas of Bur Dubai and Deira, and the stretches of beach you'll find in Jumeirah and Umm Suqeim.

Navigation

Thanks to its modern highway system, most of Dubai is fairly easy to get around. However, in some places the existing infrastructure has struggled to cope with the growth of the city, most notably Maktoum bridge spanning the Creek and the Shindagha tunnel underneath it. During rush hours (7am-9am, 1pm-2pm, 5pm-7pm Mon-Thur, Sun), some tailbacks can develop. The Business Bay bridge opened in 2007, and the floating bridge, which is open during the day, helps to ease congestion. The Salik toll system and the wider Garhoud Bridge have also helped.

People drive on the right in Dubai. Seatbelts are compulsory in the front and highly recommended in the back. In residential areas, the speed limit sits between 40kph (25mph) and 80kph (50mph). On the city highways, it is 100kph (60mph); outside the city limits it's 120kph (75mph). Road offences can lead to fines and even bans, so make sure you know all the rules. Most western licences entitle the owner to drive in a hire car for up to three months. There's a fair bit of traffic on the roads and most drivers in the city will have experienced some form of tailgating, so be as alert as possible when on the road.

Hire cars come with a Salik tag on the windscreen and costs will be added – Dhs4 for each toll gate you pass through. Even with a relatively good road system, it's best to exercise caution when driving in the city as it's known to have high numbers of road accidents, caused largely by speeding and poor lane discipline. The easiest way to get around is by taxi. Water taxis or abras are also available on the Creek and at Dubai Marina. One of the most striking aspects of getting around in Dubai is the distinct lack of an accurate system of street names. This means your destination is identified by a nearby landmark, a hotel or building. It might seem confusing at first, but you'd be surprised how quickly you get used to it.

Public transport

RTA (traffic enquiries)
800 9090, www.rta.ae

Buses

The relative convenience of taxis (and their low cost) means the public bus system is rarely used by tourists. The service is no doubt cheaper, but routes can be convoluted, so visitors often end up choosing taxis over buses just to save time. Still, if you're not in a hurry, and fancy saving some cash, you'll find timetables, prices and route maps available from the main bus stations of Al Ghubaiba in Bur Dubai and by the Gold Souk in Deira (04 227 3840). You can also call the main information line (800 9090) or visit www.rta.ae. Try to have the exact price when possible, since change for larger notes isn't easily available. Better yet, make sure you have a Nol card available at all times so you don't need to worry about carrying enough coins in your pocket. Eating, drinking and smoking are not allowed on board and the front three rows of seats are reserved for women. Passengers without tickets are liable to prosecution.

Taxis

Official taxis are well-maintained, air-conditioned and metered. A taxi will be beige with a red, green, blue or yellow roof, depending on the firm that runs it. The fare is Dhs1.6 per kilometre (0.3 miles), with a minimum Dhs10 charge regardless of the length of your trip. The two biggest firms are Dubai Transport Company (04 208 0808) and National Taxis (04 339 0002). Dubai Transport is the only company with a telephone booking system, but remember to call ahead if you've got an important appointment, especially if it's the weekend as taxis can take a while to appear. Hailing one from the street is often the easier alternative – there are usually lines of taxis waiting outside big hotels and shopping centres. If faced with an hour-long taxi queue there, head to one of the streets outside and try to flag one down. It is illegal for drivers to refuse a fare but it does happen occasionally if there's heavy traffic, so make sure to take their number down and lodge a formal complaint.

ESSENTIALS

Unofficial taxis may pull up if they see you waving. These tend to be older cars, but we'd steer clear of this option as they tend to be more expensive. Taxi drivers usually have a reasonable grasp of English, so you shouldn't find it too difficult to explain where you want to go. Fares for longer journeys outside Dubai should be agreed in advance. There is also a 12-hour service available, with petrol and driver included: call 04 208 0808. Official drivers have a reputation for returning lost items, so if you leave something in a taxi, your driver may find a way to return it to you. Failing this, call the firm you used and they will help.

Dubai Metro

The Dubai Metro opened amid much fanfare on September 9, 2009, and consists of two lines – Red and Green. All of the stations on the Red line, which runs from Rashidiya along Sheikh Zayed Road to Jebel Ali, are open. Stations on the Green line, which runs through Deira and Bur Dubai, are due to open in late 2011. You can find the latest information on the metro at www.rta.ae/dubai_metro.

There are four types of tickets you can purchase, each comes in the form of a rechargeable card. You can buy them, and even recharge them, using a ticket vending machine that can be found in every metro station. Cards start from Dhs2 for a red card, which is ideal for tourists and occasional metro users, and Dhs20 for a gold card that'll see you ride in more comfortable cabins.

Water taxis

Abras are water taxis that ferry Dubai workers and tourists across the Creek for Dhs1. The boats run between 5am and midnight, carry about 20 people, and take just a few minutes to make the crossing from Bur Dubai on the south bank of the Dubai Creek (near the textile souk) to Deira on the north side, or vice versa. A new air-conditioned water ferry operates between Deira and Dubai Marina.

Traffic fines & offences

The police website (www. dubaipolice.gov.ae) lists details of traffic violations and fines under 'Information and Procedures'. There is a zero tolerance policy in regard to drinking and driving. If you are caught driving or parking illegally by the police, you'll be issued with a mukhalifaa (fine). If clocked by a speed camera you'll normally be fined Dhs400, while jumping a red light will cost you Dhs800. When hiring a car, it's routine to sign an agreement of responsibility for any fines you may incur. To check whether you've racked up any traffic offences call 800 7777, or see www.dubaipolice.gov.ae. Fines can be paid online, or at the Muroor (Traffic Police Headquarters), near Galadari roundabout on the Dubai-Sharjah road.

Traffic accidents

If you are involved in a serious accident, call 999, but if it's just a minor collision, call the police on 04 398 1111. If you do not report scratches or bumps to the traffic police, insurers will almost certainly reject your claim. Third-party vehicle insurance is compulsory. If the accident was a minor one and no one was hurt, move the car to the side of the road and wait for the police to arrive. If there is any doubt as to who is at fault, or if there is any injury, do not move the car, even if you are blocking traffic. If you help or move anyone injured, you might be held responsible if anything happens to that person.

Breakdown services

There are two 24-hour breakdown services, the AAA (Arabian Automobile Association; 800 4900, www.aaauae.com) and IATC Recovery (International Automobile Touring Club; 800 5200, www.iatcuae.com). If you are driving when the car breaks down, pull over to the hard shoulder. The police are likely to stop and give assistance. If you're in the middle of high-speed traffic, don't get out of your car and instead call the police from the safety of your vehicle. Others include:

Auto Guard Towing Service
800 2487
Dubai Auto Towing Service
04 359 4424

Vehicle hire

Most major hire companies have offices at the airport (15 companies operate, some of which are open 24 hours a day) and hotels. Before renting a car, check the small print, especially clauses relating to insurance cover in the event of an accident, as this can vary considerably from company to company. Drivers must be over 21 to hire a small car, or 25 for a medium (two-litre) or larger 4x4 vehicle. You'll need your national driving licence (an International Driving Permit is best, although it isn't legally required). You'll also need your passport and a major credit card. Prices range from Dhs160 per day for a small automatic car to Dhs1,400 for something like a Lexus LS460 or a much beloved 4x4. Motorbikes are not available for hire in Dubai. Some car rental firms:

Autolease *04 282 6565*,
www.autolease-uae.com
Avis *04 295 7121*,
www.avisuae.ae
Budget *04 295 6667*,
www.budget-uae.com
Diamond Lease *04 885 2677*,
www.diamondlease.com
Europe *04 223 7911*,
www.europcar.com
Hertz *800 43789*,
www.hertz-uae.com
Thrifty *800 4694*,
www.thriftyuae.com

Fuel stations

At the time of writing, the cost of petrol was between Dhs80-100 to fill a tank. There are 24-hour petrol stations on all major highways and most have convenience stores selling snacks or are attached to various fast food restaurants.

Parking

Many areas in the city have now introduced paid parking to reduce congestion, with inspectors conducting regular patrols. Prices are quite reasonable (Dhs2 for a one-hour stay, depending on location) and they are known to operate only at peak times (usually from 8am to noon and 4pm to 9pm). It's free to park outside these hours on Fridays and public holidays. Parking tickets are common though, so keep an eye on the time.

Road signs

Road signs are in English and Arabic, which makes it easier for Westerners. But the sheer scale of the American-style highway system (up to six lanes on either side) means it's best to always stay alert, especially at the junctions on Sheikh Zayed Road that have multiple exits and little warnings.

ESSENTIALS

Resources A-Z

Accidents & emergencies

Call the following for the emergency services:

Police 999
Fire 997
Ambulance 998/999
Coastguard 04 345 0260

If you dial 999 in an emergency, Dubai Police can sometimes send a helicopter if there is a bad accident. Dubai has well-equipped public and private hospitals but while emergency care for all UAE nationals, visitors and expatriates is free from the Al Wasl, New Dubai and Rashid hospitals, all other treatments at hospitals and doctors are charged to tourists, so it's advisable to have comprehensive both medical and travel insurance before you travel to the city.

Al Wasl Hospital
Oud Metha Road, south of Al Qataiyat Road, Za'abeel (04 324 1111).
American Hospital Dubai
*Off Oud Metha **Road** between Lamcy Plaza & Wafi Centre, Al Nasr, Bur Dubai (04 336 7777).*
Emirates Hospital
Opposite Jumeirah Beach Park, next to Chili's restaurant, Beach Road, Jumeirah (04 349 6666).
Iranian Hospital
Corner of Al Hudeiba Road & Al Wasl Road, Satwa (04 344 0250).
New Dubai Hospital
Opposite Hamria Vegetable Market, after Hyatt Regency Hotel, Deira (04 271 4444).
Rashid Hospital
Oud Metha Road, nr Al Maktoum Bridge, Bur Dubai (04 337 4000).

Welcare Hospital
Next to Lifco supermarket in Garhoud, Deira (04 282 7788).

Customs

There is a duty-free shop in the airport arrivals hall. Each person is permitted to bring into the UAE four litres of spirits or two cartons of beer, 400 cigarettes, 50 cigars and 500g of tobacco. No customs duty is levied on personal effects which are brought into Dubai. For more explanations on duty levied on particular products, visit the website at www.dubaiairport.com, or call 04 224 5555.

The following goods are prohibited in the UAE and importing these items will incur a heavy penalty: controlled substances (drugs), firearms and ammunition, pornography (including sex toys), unstrung pearls, pork, raw seafood and fruit and vegetables that come from cholera-infected areas. Some recent high-profile cases (including arrests for prescription painkillers and fractions of a gram of hashish) have highlighted just how seriously smuggling is taken here. For further information, see the 'Travelers Guide' posted on the website www. dxbcustoms.gov.ae.

Dental

Good dentists are readily available, but prices can be hefty. Dubai Smile Dental Centre offers 24-hour emergency care.

Dr Michael's Dental Clinic
04 349 5900, www.drmichaels.com
Dubai Smile Dental Centre
04 398 6662, www.dubaismile.com

Drs. Nicolas & Asp
04 394 7777, www.nicolasandasp.com

Disabled

Although things are beginning to improve, many places are still not equipped to facilitate wheelchair access. Most hotels have made token efforts at improving their facilities, but functionality still plays second fiddle to design. Those hotels that do have specially adapted rooms include the Burj Al Arab, City Centre Hotel, Crowne Plaza, Jumeirah Emirates Towers, Hilton Dubai Creek, Hilton Dubai Jumeirah, Hyatt Regency, Jumeirah Beach Hotel, JW Marriott, Oasis Beach Hotel, Madinat Jumeirah, Ritz-Carlton Dubai, Renaissance, One&Only Royal Mirage. The airport and major shopping centres such as the Mall of the Emirates have good wheelchair access. Some Dubai Transport taxis are fitted to accommodate wheelchairs. For more details, call their number 04 208 0808.

Electricity

The domestic electricity supply is 220/240 volts AC, 50Hz. Sockets are suitable for three-pin 13 amp plugs of British standard design. It is a good idea to bring an adaptor with you to Dubai, as some buildings have two-pin sockets. Adaptors can be purchased cheaply in local supermarkets. Appliances that are bought in the UAE will have two-pin plugs attached. For more information, call the Ministry of Electricity on 04 262 6262.

Embassies & consulates

For information about passport, visa, commercial and consular services, press and public affairs, contact your country's embassy or consulate. If you need to contact an official urgently, don't despair: there is often a number on the embassy's answer service, which you can call for help outside working hours.

Australian Consulate
1st floor, Emirates Atrium Building, Sheikh Zayed Road, (04 508 7100, www.austrade.gov.au). **Open** 8am-3.30pm Mon-Wed, Sun; 8am-2.45pm Thur.

Canadian Consulate
17 floor, Juma Al Bhaji Building, Bank Street, Bur Dubai (04 314 5555, www.dfait-maeci.gc.ca). **Open** 8am-4pm Mon-Thur, Sun.

French Consulate
18th floor, API World Tower, Sheikh Zayed Road (04 332 9040, www.consulfrance-dubai.org.ae). **Open** 8.30am-1pm, Mon-Thur, Sun.

Indian Consulate
Al Hamria Diplomatic Enclave, Consulate area, nr BurJuman Centre (04 397 1333, www.cgidubai.com). **Open** 8am-4.30pm Mon-Thur, Sun.

Pakistani Consulate
Khalid bin Waleed Road, nr BurJuman Centre (04 397 3600). **Open** 7.30am-noon Mon-Thur, Sun.

Republic of Ireland Consulate
1301 Crown Plaza Commercial Tower Sheikh Zayed Road (04 331 4215, www.embassyofireland.org.sa). **Open** 9am-1pm Mon-Thur, Sun.

South African Consulate
Dubai Islamic Bank Building, Bur Dubai (04 397 5222, www.southafrica.ae). **Open** 8am-4pm Mon-Thur, Sun.

UK Consulate
British Embassy Building, Al Seef Road, Bur Dubai (04 309 4444, www.britain-uae.org). **Open** 7.30am-2.30pm Mon-Thur, Sun.

US Consulate
21st floor, Dubai World Trade Centre, Sheikh Zayed Road (04 311 6000, www.dubai.usconsulate.gov). **Open** 8.30am-5pm Mon-Thur, Sun.

ESSENTIALS

Internet

Most hotels have good access, but sites that fall under 'prohibited categories' are blocked. These include any that are 'inconsistent with the religious, cultural, political and moral values of the United Arab Emirates'. So no online poker, dating or overt criticism of the government, and no cheap international phone calls. Internet cafés are clustered in Khalid bin Waleed (Computer) Street in Bur Dubai and in parts of Deira, Karama and Satwa. Otherwise, have a coffee or snack and surf for free at these coffee shops around town:

Caribou Coffee
Academic City, Al Ghurair City, DIFC, Festival City, Garhoud Views, JBR, Marina Mall, Mirdif, Souk Al Bahar, The Dubai Mall, The Greens/The Views, Times Square Centre, WAFI (04 427 0543).
Caffè Nero
DIFC, Green Community, Jumeirah Lakes Towers, Motor City, The Dubai Mall (04 339 9731, www.caffenero.com/uae).
Elements Café
WAFI, Oud Metha (04 324 4252).

Opening hours

The working week runs from Sunday to Thursday. Working hours are typically 9am to 6pm, but a few firms still operate a split-shift system (normally 8am-noon and 4pm-8pm). Malls tend to open from 10am to 10pm on weekdays and 10am to midnight on weekends.

Police

In the case of an emergency, call 999. If you just want information, www.dubaipolice.gov.ae is a good resource. If you want to report something confidentially or think you have witnessed something illegal, call Al Ameen Service on 800 4888, or go to www.alameen.ae.

Post

The UAE's post is run solely by Empost, and works on a PO Box system, although a postal delivery service is planned for the future. Hotels will handle mail for guests and you can buy stamps at post offices, Emarat petrol stations and card shops. Shopping malls, such as Mercato, have postal facilities. Delivery takes between two and three days within the UAE, but up to 10 days (or more) for deliveries to Europe and the US. The service can be erratic, so don't be surprised if delivery takes longer than planned. All postal enquiries can be directed to the Empost call centre on 600 599 999 (7am-10pm Mon-Thur, Sat, Sun). Alternatively, call the Emirates Post Head Office on 04 262 2222 (7am-10pm daily).

Central Post Office
Za'abeel Road, Karama (04 337 1500, www.empostuae.com). **Open** 8am-10pm Mon-Thur, Sat, Sun.

Smoking

A smoking ban came into force in January 2008, which has made all Dubai restaurants non-smoking indoors. Smoking is still permitted in bars and outdoors on terraces. Indoor smoking is permitted if the restaurant has a designated room, but most don't.

Telephones

The international dialling code for the UAE is 971, followed by the individual emirate's code. For Dubai, this is 04. Other area codes are as follows: Abu Dhabi 02, Ajman 06, Al Ain 03, Fujairah 09,

Ras Al Khaimah 07 and Sharjah 06. For mobile telephones, the code is 050, 055 or 056. Drop the initial '0' of these codes if dialling from abroad. Operator services can be contacted on 100; directory enquiries are available on 181, or 151 for international numbers. Alternatively, consult the Yellow Pages directory online at www.yellowpages.ae, which in many cases can be much quicker and far less frustrating.

Making a call

Until fairly recently, Etisalat (www.etisalat.com) had a monopoly on all telecommunications in the UAE, but 2006 saw the launch of rival company Du (www.du.ae), which offers some competition, especially in the mobile phone market. Local calls are very inexpensive, and direct dialling is available to more than 100 countries. Pay phones, which are both card- and coin-operated, are located throughout the UAE. To make a call within Dubai, dial the seven-digit phone number; for calls to other regions within the UAE, dial the area code followed by the seven-digit phone number. To make an international call, dial 00, then the appropriate country code (Australia 61; Canada 1; France 33; India 91; New Zealand 64; the Republic of Ireland 353; South Africa 27; Pakistan 92; Russia 7; UK 44; US 1;). Next, dial the area code, omitting the initial 0, followed by the telephone number.

Public telephones

There are plenty of public telephones, which accept either cash or phone cards. Cards for local and international use are available in various denominations (including Dhs25 and Dhs50) from most

supermarkets and shopping malls. Coin-operated phones accept Dhs1 and 50 fils coins.

Mobile telephones

Dubai has one of the world's highest rates of mobile phone usage and practically everyone has at least one cellular phone. A reciprocal agreement exists with over 60 countries, allowing GSM international roaming service for other networks in the UAE. You can pick up visitor mobile plans at the Dubai International Airport. Etisalat's 'Ahlan' plan costs just Dhs60, with Dhs25 worth of credit, it's valid for 90 days. In comparison, Du's Visitor Mobile Line costs just Dhs49 and includes Dhs20 credit.

Tickets

Tickets can often be bought from the venue or on the door, but it's wise to book ahead for any major gigs. Visit the *Time Out* ticket line (800 4669, www.timeoutdubai.com). They can also be picked up from *Time Out*'s ticket office in Media City (behind Building 14).

Time

The UAE is four hours ahead of GMT and has no seasonal change. For instance, if it is noon in London (winter time), it is 4pm in Dubai; when British clocks move forwards for BST, noon in the UK is 3pm in Dubai.

Tipping

Hotels and restaurants usually include a 15 per cent service charge in the bill; if not, adding ten per cent is normal, if not obligatory. Unfortunately, this inclusive charge usually goes straight to the restaurant and rarely reaches the pockets of the people who served you; so if you are particularly impressed with the service, you will need to tip in addition to the inclusive total. It is common to pay taxi drivers a small tip: rounding up the taxi fare to the nearest Dhs5 is the norm. For other services, includin gthose of supermarket baggers, petrol pump attendants and hoetl valets, it is usual to give at least a couple of dirhams.

Tourist information

The Department of Tourism & Commerce Marketing (DTCM) is the government's sole regulating, planning and licensing body for the tourism industry in Dubai. It has information centres dotted around the city, the most useful being located in the airport arrivals lounge (04 224 5252).

These one-stop information centres aim to answer any visitor queries, provide maps, tour guides and hotel information, as well as business and conference advice. Most of the larger shopping malls have their own centres providing visitor information.

Department of Tourism & Commerce Marketing
10th-12th floor, National Bank of Dubai Building, Baniyas Road, Deira (04 223 0000, www. dubaitourism.ae). **Open** 7.30am-2.30pm Mon-Thur, Sun.

Visas

Visa regulations are always liable to change, so it is worth checking them with your travel agent or the UAE embassy in your home country before leaving. Overstaying your visa can result in detention and fines. Nationals of Israel may not enter the UAE. Your passport must have at least two months (in some

cases six) left before expiry for you to be granted admission to the UAE, so make sure you check before booking your flight.

UK
Citizens of the UK will be granted a free visit visa on arrival in the UAE: passports will be stamped with the visa as you pass through immigration. The visa is usually stamped for a month and may be extended for another 30 day period for Dhs700.

Multiple-entry visas
Multiple-entry visas are available to business visitors who have a relationship with either a multinational company or a reputable local business, and who visit the UAE regularly. This type of visa is valid for six months from the date of issue and the maximum duration of each stay is 30 days. The cost of such a visa is Dhs1,000. The visitor must enter the UAE on a visit visa and obtain the multiple entry visa while in the country. The visa is stamped in the passport.

96-hour visa for transit passengers
As a way of promoting Dubai's city tours, passengers from Europe, US, Asia and Africa who stopover for a minimum of five hours are eligible for a free 96-hour transit visa, which enables them to go into the city. This visa is available only to those travelling onwards from Dubai.

What's on

Time Out Dubai is available from all good newsagents and supermarkets and comes out every Wednesday. The magazine contains comprehensive listings and reviews on entertainment-related places in the city, as well as all the restaurants and spas you'll need.

ESSENTIALS

A tailor's shop in Deira

Vocabulary

Arabic is the official language of Dubai although both Urdu and Hindi are widely spoken, but English is all you'll need to get by if you're only coming for a short visit. That said, using a few Arabic phrases is always appreciated and goes a long way in impressing locals. Some basic words and phrases are given below, written phonetically. Capitals are not used in Arabic, but they are used below to indicate hard sounds.

Useful phrases

hello marhaba
how are you? kaif il haal? **good morning** sabaaH il khayr
good evening masaa' il khayr
greetings 'as-salamu 'alaykum
goodbye ma' 'is-salaama
excuse me afwan
sorry 'aasif
God willing insha'allah
please (to a man) min fadlak, (to a woman) min fadlik
thank you (very much) shukran (jazeelan)
yes/no na'am/laa
don't know lasto adree or laa 'a-arif
who?/what? man?/matha?
where?/why? ayina?/lematha?
how much? (cost) bekam?
how many? kam?
The bill, please alfatourah min faDlak.
do you speak English? 'I'itkallam inglizi
I don't speak Arabic maatkallam arabi
nice to meet you yusadni moqapalatak
what's your name? ma esmok?
my name is... esmei...
how old are you? kam amrk?
what's your job?/where do you work? ma heya wazefatuk?/ayna tam'al?
where do you live? ayna taskun?
I live/ I work in Dubai askun/ a'amal fi Dubai
how is the family? Kayfa halou l'a ila?
congratulations mabrook
with pleasure bikul siroor
have a good trip atmna lak rehla muafaqa
thanks for coming shukran limajee, ak
best wishes atyab al-tamniyat
when will I see you? mata sa'araak?
wait a little intazarni kaliln
calm down hadia nafsak;
can I help you? hl astateea'i musaa'adatuk?

Numbers & time

0 sifr; **1** waahid; **2** itnain; **3** talata; **4** arba'a; **5** khamsa; **6** sitta; **7** sab'a; **8** tamanya; **9** tis'a; **10** 'ashra; **100** me'ah; **Sunday** al-ahad; **Monday** al-itnayn; **Tuesday** al-talata; **Wednesday** al-arba'a; **Thursday** al-khamees; **Friday** al-jum'a; **Saturday** al-Sabt; **day** yom; **month** shahr; **year** sanah; **hour** sa'aa; **minute** daqiqa; **today** al yom; **yesterday** ams/imbarah; **tomorrow** bukra

Getting around

airport *matar*; **post office** *maktab al barid*; **bank** *bank*; **passport** *jawaz safar*; **luggage** *'aghraud*, **ticket** *tath karah*; **taxi** *taxi*; **car** *say-yarra*; **city** *madina*; **street** *share'h*; **road** *tareeq*; **bridge** *jisr*; **mosque** *jame'h* or *messjed*; **bazaar** *souk*; **boat** *markab*; **beach** *il-shat'i*; **customs** *jumrok*; **library** *maktabeh*;

Menu Glossary

Arayes: Deep-fried lamb sandwich

Baba ghanoush: Chargrilled eggplant, tahini, olive oil, lemon juice and garlic served as a dip or an altenative to hoummus

Baharat: Arabic mixed spices

Baklava: Dessert of layered pastry filled with nuts and steeped in honey-lemon syrup – usually cut into triangular or diamond shapes

Burghul: Parboiled and dried wheat kernels processed into grain, used in taboulech and mixed with lamb in kibbeh

Ejje: Arabic omelette

Falafel: Small deep-fried patties made of generously-spiced ground chickpeas

Fatayer: Pastry pockets filled with spinach, meat or cheese

Fattoush: Salad of croutons, cucumber, tomato and mint

Haleeb: Milk

Hammour: Red Sea fish of the grouper family

Kabsa: Classic Arabian dish of meat mixed with rice

Kibbeh: Oval-shaped nuggets of ground lamb and burghul

Koshary: Cooked dish of pasta, rice and lentils to which, onions, chillis and tomato paste are added

Kufta: Fingers, balls or a flat cake of minced meat and spices that may be baked or charcoal grilled on skewers

Laban: Tangy-tasting sour milk drink widely used in cooking as a substitute for milk

Labneh: Thick, creamy cheese, often spiced and used as a dip

Lahma bi ajeen: Arabic pizza

Ma'amul: Date cookies shaped in a wooden mould called a *tabi*

Makloubeh: Meat or fish with rice, broad beans and cauliflower

Mantou: Dumplings stuffed with minced lamb

Mouhammara: Mixture of ground nuts, olive oil, cumin and chillis, eaten with Arabic bread

Moutabel: Aubergine dip made with tahini, olive oil and lemon juice

Rocca: Aromatic green salad with a peppery, mustard flavour, used in salads or mixed with hot yoghurt

Sambusek: Triangular pies filled with meat, cheese or spinach

Sayyadiya: Delicately-spiced fish dish served on a bed of rice

Shaour: Red Sea fish from the emperor family

Shawarma: A cone of pressed lamb, chicken or beef roasted on a vertical spit. Meat is shaved off from the outside while the spit is turning. Also can mean Arabic bread filled with shawarma meat, salad, hot sauce and tahini

Shisha: Pipe for smoking tobacco leaves or dried fruit through a water filter. Also known as a hubbly bubbly or hookah pipe

Shish taouk: Skewered chicken pieces cooked over charcoal. Often served with chips

Shourba: Soup

Snober: Pine nuts

Sumac: Ground powder from the cashew family, used as a seasoning

Tabouleh: Salad of burghul, tomato, mint and parsley

Tahini: An oily paste made from ground sesame seeds, used in hommus, moutabel and baba ghanoush

Taratour: A thick mayonnaise of puréed pine nuts, garlic and lemon, used as a sauce or dip

Umm ali: 'Ali's mother' is a locally devised pastry pudding with raisins and coconut, steeped in milk

Warak enab: Stuffed vine leaves

Zatoon: Olives

Zattar: Blend of spices including thyme, sumac and marjoram

Index

ESSENTIALS

ESSENTIALS

Distinctly different Thai

BLUERAIN